齐白石 Qi Baishi:

An Introduction to his Life and Art

by

Thomas Hayes

and

李思瑾 Li Sijin

First published in Great Britain 2017 by Mirador Publishing.

Copyright © 2017 Thomas Hayes and Li Sijin.

All rights reserved. No part of this publication may be reproduced, distributed or transmitted in any form or by any means, including photocopying, recording or other electronic or mechanical methods, without the prior written permission of the publisher, except in the case of brief quotations embodied in critical reviews and certain other non-commercial uses permitted by copyright law. For permission requests, write to the publisher at the address below.

ISBN: 978-1-912192-75-5

A copy of this work is available through the British Library.

Mirador Publishing
10 Greenbrook Terrace
Taunton
Somerset
TA1 1UT

Table of Contents

ACKNOWLEDGEMENTS 1

ABOUT THE AUTHORS 2

INTRODUCTION 4

CHAPTER ONE: A SUMMARY OF THE LIFE OF QI BAISHI 1

CHAPTER TWO: THE WORKS OF QI BAISHI 1 17

    1. THREE FISH 17

    2. LYCHEE AND SQUIRREL 19

    3. COCKSCOMB AND CHICKS 21

    4. BEGONIAS 23

    5. CABBAGE AND GRASSHOPPER 25

    6. FORTUNATE MANDARIN DUCKS 27

    7. YANLAIHONG (YOUNG OLD MAN) AND DRAGONFLY 29

    8. CHRYSANTHEMUM AND TWO BIRDS 31

    9. SHRIMP 1 33

    10. SHRIMP 2 35

    11. CUSHAWS 37

    12. PEACHES, POMEGRANATES AND DRAGONFLY 39

    13. LYCHEE 41

    14. LOTUS 43

CHAPTER THREE: THE WORKS OF QI BAISHI 2 45

    1. CHICKS AND MORNING GLORIES 45

    2. CHRYSANTHEMUM AND LONGEVITY 47

    3. LONGEVITY 1 49

    4. WISTERIA 51

    6. LOOFAH 55

    7. MORNING GLORIES AND DRAGONFLY 57

    8. MAGNOLIA FLOWER 59

    9. LOTUS 61

    10. LONGEVITY 2 63

    11. LUCID GANODERMA 65

    12. PEONY AND VASE 67

    13. CHRYSANTHEMUM AND AUTUMN INSECT 69

CHAPTER FOUR: THE WORKS OF QI BAISHI 3 71

1. QI BAOZHU 71
2. LIGHT 73
3. DINGCHAO 75
4. MODESTY 77
5. TOOL BOX 79
6. THE BED FRAME 81
7. CARVED STONE AND BAMBOO 83

IMAGE 4-7: CARVED STONE AND BAMBOO 83

CHAPTER FIVE: PABLO PICASSO 84

CHAPTER SIX: PABLO PICASSO AND QI BAISHI – A COMPARISON 90

CHAPTER SEVEN: THE QI BAISHI MUSEUM IN XIANGTAN 100

Acknowledgements

We are especially grateful to Sarah and her team at Mirador Publishing. They have worked quickly and efficiently in publishing this book. As always, they have been both flexible and courteous, acting with tenacity and good grace at all times. Without the contribution of the great Qi Baishi and Picasso, alongside other countless great artists, this book would not be possible.

About the Authors

Thomas Hayes

Thomas Hayes has studied and practised the Daoist Arts for more than thirty years. In addition to practising Chen-style Tàijíquán and Qigong, he studies the Yìjīng and other associated Chinese Daoist and Buddhist metaphysical systems and has practised other Buddhist, Advaita Vedanta and Yoga traditions. He has qualifications in Stress Management, Life Coaching, Hypnotherapy and NLP. He is also a qualified TEFL teacher.

Thomas works as a freelance consultant in information management and is a Fellow of the British Computer Society. He never ceases to learn and practise, and has a lifelong devotion to self-cultivation. He has been visiting Xiangtan for twenty years and has many friends there.

Thomas also works as a consultant to Chinese businesses and acts a bridge between Western and Chinese culture. On his last trip to China in October 2016 he met Li Sijin and they decided to undertake the production of this work. This is his second collaborative book. His first book, *Chen Tàijíquán: The Theory and Practice of a Daoist Internal Martial Art: Volume 1 – Basics and Short Form*, was also published by Mirador Publishing in 2016.

Thomas lives in Manchester, England.

李思瑾 Li Sijin

李思瑾 Li Sijin has worked as an art expert at the Qi Baishi Memorial Hall in her home town of Xiangtan City, Hunan, for the last nine years. She shares her hometown origins of Xiangtan with the subject of this book: 齐白石 Qi Baishi. She has undertaken the detailed analysis of the subject and has also injected much needed effort and commensurate enthusiasm into the production of this book. She 'lives and breathes' the subject and regards herself as fortunate that she has a job that she regards equally as a calling.

Li Sijin is also a practising accountant and a Master of Ceremonies. Therefore, she is a woman with wide-ranging skills and talents. She is especially interested in promoting the works of Qi Baishi and traditional Chinese culture in general to a Western audience. One of the interesting things that she became aware of when she welcomed Western visitors to the Qi Baishi Museum in Xiangtan was that hardly anyone had heard of Qi Baishi and yet almost everyone had heard of Picasso. This provided an additional reason for her to write this book and to spread the word about the genius and his prodigious works to a wider audience.

Introduction

Our aim in writing this short, introductory book is a simple one: to provide to a Western audience a sample of the works of Qi Baishi and to include some background to the man himself. The book has been written as a result of a special collaboration between two authors: an English man and a Chinese woman, both of whom have connections with Qi Baishi's home town. Although they are from different generations, cultures and countries, they both have a reverence for all art. They have also been inspired to write this book as a result of their intense interest in the specific subject of Qi Baishi, together with that of a wider appreciation for traditional Chinese art in general.

In writing this book we have used Chinese characters sparingly and only where appropriate in order to avoid adding an unnecessary level of language complexity. For example, 齐白石 is the name of Qi Baishi as expressed in Chinese characters. The writing of his name in the format of Qi Baishi is derived from the adoption of the Pinyin system of transliteration that is now widely used in China. This system is used to represent in literal form how the Chinese characters sound.

Qi is the family name (surname), and precedes the chosen name, Baishi or Bai Shi. This is of course, opposite to the Western method where the surname is written after the chosen name(s). The Pinyin can be written as two separate words – Bai Shi, or as a concatenation – Baishi. We have chosen the latter method for simplicity rather than conformity, and this method is adopted for this and other Pinyin words used. Bai and Shi are Qi's two forenames. Thus, his full name can also be written as Qi Bai Shi.

A further potential cause of confusion is that the Chinese may use the day of the

Chinese New Year as the start date for their age. Moreover, this date varies each year, like Easter in the West. In addition, the Chinese sometimes also count their age as 1, from the year of birth. So, a person who has reached the first anniversary of their birth date may be regarded as being 2 years old. Again, for the purposes of simplicity we have adopted the Western method.

There is a further level of complexity with regards to Qi Baishi. This may cause confusion when aligning his age with his works, and for this reason it needs to be explained. In the year of, and prior to his death in 1957, he declared himself to be 97 years old. Of course, being born in 1864, his real age was 93. So, there is a discrepancy of four years.

Qi Baishi claimed that he was born two years into the Qing dynasty. This is a lunar year in China and was different to the modern calendar of today. The year was 1863 in the lunar year calculation at that time, but it is 1864 by today's reckoning. So, Qi said that he was born on 22 November 1863. Furthermore, as stated above, the Chinese used to calculate the year of birth starting at 1. So, on the first anniversary of one's birth you would be 2 years old.

In addition, when Qi was in Changsha, the capital of Hunan province and close to Xiangtan, a fortune teller told him that it would be difficult for him to live beyond 75 years of age. This was in 1937. He took this statement very seriously and so closed himself off from the world and stayed at home. He didn't meet anyone during that period, even his family.

After having survived what he considered to be a very dangerous time, he took the fortune teller's advice and added a further two years to his age. He then claimed that he was 77 years old. So, this was an additional two years added to the one year added from using the year 1863 as his birth date from the Chinese lunar method and the one year added from starting to count his date of birth as 1 year old.

For the ease of simplicity, we shall use the modern, Western method of calculation when and where we state his age. Of course, you need to be aware that different ages may be used by others (including Qi Baishi) when stating how old he was at the time he produced individual works of art.

Within his native China, Qi Baishi is an esteemed and very famous artist. His works are still highly prized today, despite his death some sixty years ago, in 1957. On 25 February 2010, the British newspaper, the *Daily Telegraph*, reported that he had become the world's third best-ever selling artist, behind Andy Warhol and Pablo Picasso. In 2011, one of his paintings sold at auction for almost $66 million.

Qi Baishi was born into poverty and spent much of his early life as a member of a peasant family. He also received no formal artistic training at any school or university. His use of water paintings, bringing to life subjects such as mice, birds and shrimp, are part of the Chinese classical artistic tradition into which he was born and raised. To have painted or drawn mice was very rare in the Chinese classical artistic tradition at that time. Qi very much believed in painting subjects that ordinary people could relate to and understand.

The book is meant to be a short introduction and nothing more. If we can achieve, with this modest contribution, an introduction to Qi Baishi to those who are unaware of his works and who will appreciate what they see, then we will feel that we have accomplished what we set out to do.

In order to create a bridge between Western and Asian styles, we offer a short introduction to the works of Pablo Picasso and provide a brief comparison between the two artists. This is merely to provide some context for a Western audience by introducing a well-known Western artist who had many similarities with Qi Baishi. They both lived into old age, lived during turbulent times and rose to the very top of their artistic realms. Remaining consistent, our ambition is not to provide an extensive analysis, but merely to provide a very high-level summary and comparison.

Qi Baishi and Pablo Picasso were both prodigious artists, who continued with their work right up until the end of their lives. They also were peace advocates and felt the suffering of the violent times that they lived in. More significantly, both rose to the very highest level of greatness. If they lived in today's modern times, I am sure that they would meet up frequently. During the era that they lived in, the two hemispheres of the world were very separate, with unsophisticated communication and travel making interaction unlikely.

All the information provided in this book about Qi Baishi, both in terms of his life and his works, has been obtained from original source documents and materials from the archives held in the Qi Baishi Museum in his home town of Xiantang.

Chapter One: A Summary of the Life of Qi Baishi

This chapter provides a very brief sketch of the life of Qi Baishi. In English, his forenames 'Bai' and 'Shi' are from two separate words that translate into English as 'white stone'.

It is very difficult to provide a very detailed history of his life. This is first and foremost due to the extreme political turbulence that existed in China during that period. Consequently, there is a lack of adequate historical record-keeping. Also, as stated in the Introduction, it is not our intention in this short book to provide anything other than a brief outline of his life and work and to let the images of his work speak for themselves.

Qi Baishi also was known by many other names such as 齐纯芝 Qi Chunzhi and 渭青 Wei Qing. He also had many other pseudonyms such as 齐璜 Qi Huang、白石山人 Baishi Shan Ren、and 齐大 QI Da.

Qi adopted a 'playful' style with his paintings, balancing two objectives: that of achieving an exact likeness and that of applying his own individual artistic licence. While he maintained his own style, he was definitely from the Chinese tradition and therefore was not influenced by any Western artists. He applied his own unique method, derived from the precedents of the Chinese artistic tradition. He stated, "When speaking, use language that people can understand. When painting, depict things that people have seen."

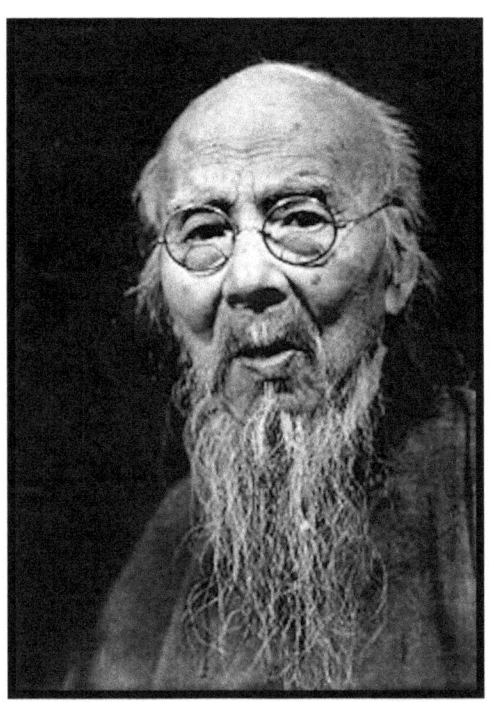

Image 1-1: 齐白石 Qi Baishi

On 1 January 1864, Qi Baishi was born into a peasant family in Xiangtan county, Hunan province, China. This is the same part of China that the country's famous leader, Chairman Mao Ze Dong, originated from. The two men would meet later in their lives. Hunan is a mountainous province situated in southern China. In English 'Hunan' means 'south of the lake'.

Hunan is also the home town of Zhou Shiyi, the author of *The Kinship of the Three, According to the Book of Changes*; a translation of the famous Chinese Daoist internal alchemy classic by Wei Boyang. Robert Peng, who is now a famous Qigong healer in the West (and who treated Rupert Murdoch) also originated from Xiangtan. The above are but a few; more could be mentioned. Therefore, the town of Hunan has provided an ongoing source of genius throughout the generations.

Qi Baishi lived and grew up with all of his family: that is, his parents, grandparents and five brothers. He was the eldest of the siblings. From a young age, he suffered from poor health and therefore did not have the strength and stamina required to help his family with the back-breaking manual labour that went with farming the land.

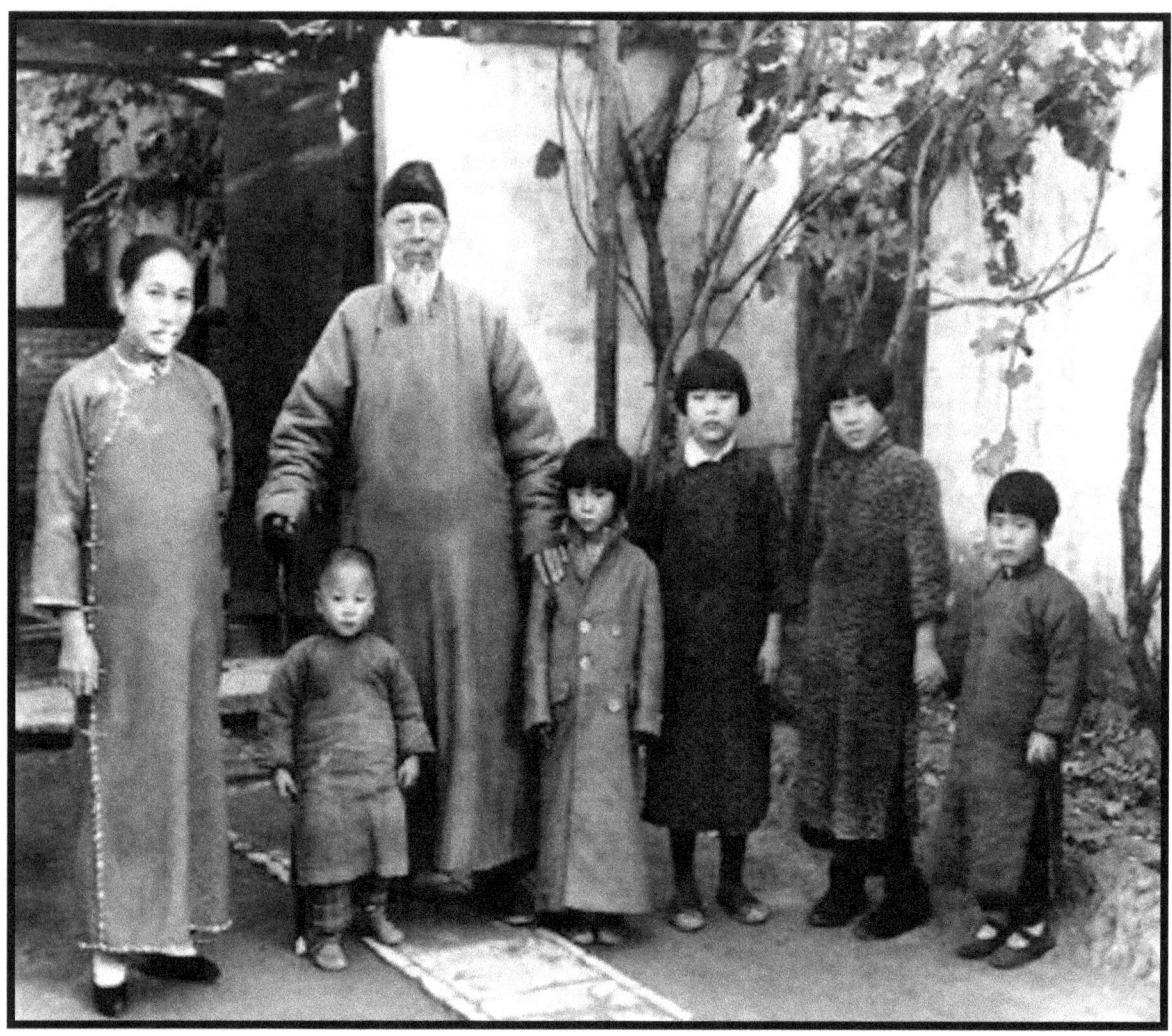

Image 1-2: Qi Baishi with his wife and children

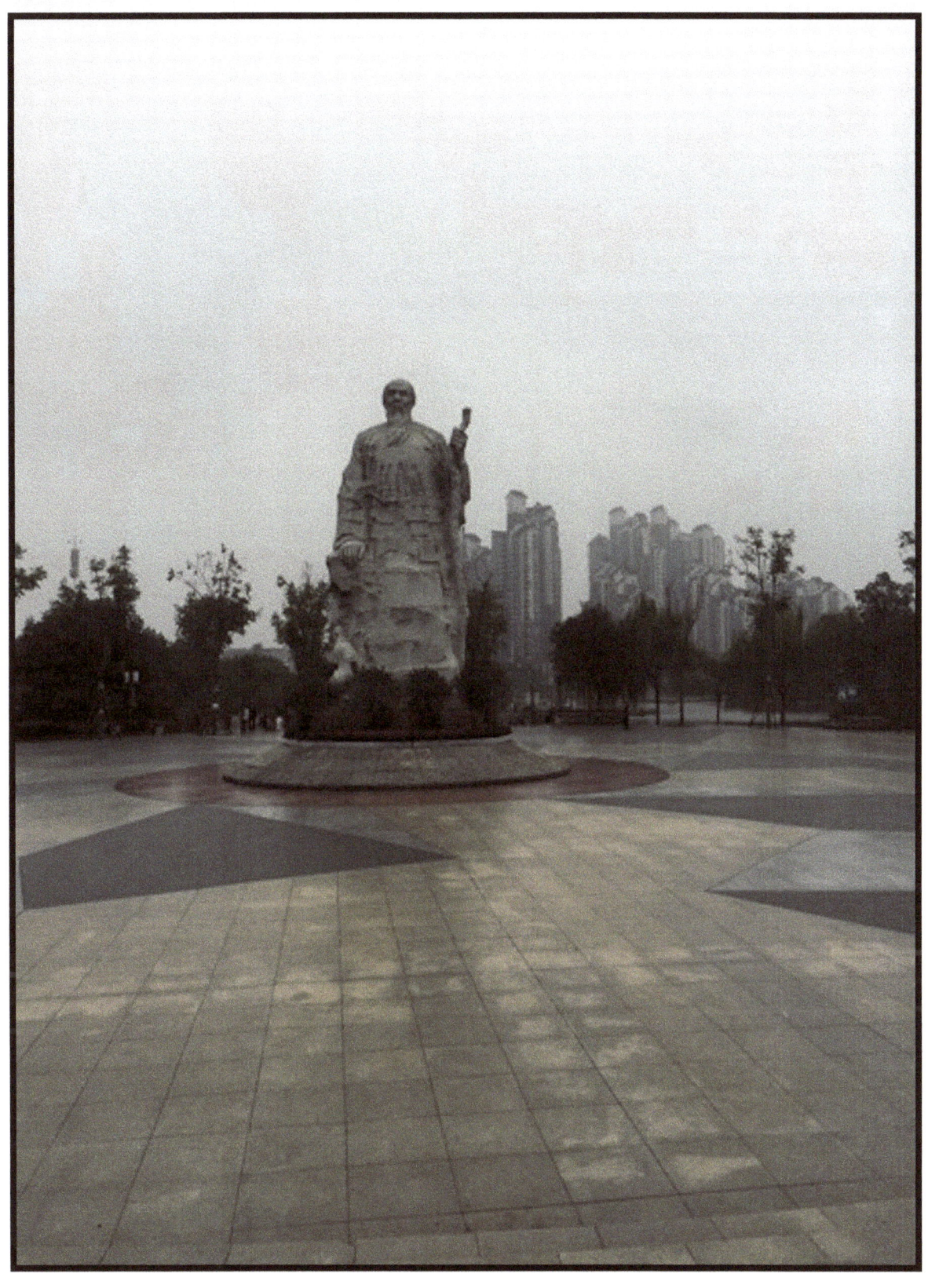

Image 1-3: Qi Baishi statue in the park named after him in Xiangtan, Hunan

The year of his birth, 1864, coincided with the end of the Taiping rebellion against the Manchu Qing dynasty. This civil strife started in 1851 and lasted for fourteen years. It was one of the bloodiest periods of violence in human history, and the numbers of deaths can be counted in the millions. Hence, Qi was born during very turbulent times, even by the standards of Chinese history. Thereafter, his life span covered a period of further huge political upheaval: the demise of the Qing dynasty; the establishment of the Republic of China; two world wars; the rise of the Chinese Communist Party; and the Korean War. He certainly lived during the 'interesting times'; said to be a type of mixed blessing attributed to the Chinese. Nevertheless, he maintained his own style and artistic expression and was not diverted by any of these violent events.

In 1870, at just 6 years of age, Qi was taught by his grandfather in the latter's private school in his home town of Xiangtan. He then dropped out of the school approximately six months later. In 1878, when he was 14 years of age, he learned simple carpentry and became a pupil of Zhou Zhimei, learning how to fashion basic designs. During his formative years, he discovered a Chinese manual of painting known as 芥子园画谱 *Jieziyuan Huapu, the Mustard Seed Garden Manual of Painting*. This was a late seventeenth-century production which generated within him an intense interest in art, and consequently he taught himself how to paint. When he was 16, he studied with Zhou Zhimei, a woodcarver.

In 1881, as a young man of just 17 years of age, he married his first wife, Chen Chunjun (1863–1940). He was at that time working as a carpenter and travelled the countryside, going from door to door with his teacher to undertake work. In order to make ends meet, he continued with this type of work over the next few years.

In 1888, at 24 years of age, Qi decided to become an artist and was adopted as a pupil by Xiao Xianggai, from whom he learned how to draw portraits. At that time, there was a growing demand for portrait paintings, and Xiao Xianggai was regarded as the best artist of his generation in Xiangtan.

The following year, Qi became a pupil of Hu Qinyuan, who taught him how to use the combination of fine brushwork and attention to detail, known as the 'gongbi method'. This is a stylised brush technique that is precise and without variation and is used for more descriptive rather than interpretive paintings.

Chen Shaofan, a teacher of literature, taught Qi how to write poetry. Under the direction of Hu Qinyuan, he then gave up carpentry and focused all his efforts on painting.

In 1894, at just 30 years of age, Qi became the president of Long Shan Shi She, the Dragon Hill Poetry Society and then later Luo Shan Shi She, the Longshan Poetry Society. These were two societies founded by Qi and his friends in Xiangtan. At this time he was therefore devoting his time to three artistic pursuits: poetry, painting and seal-making. So, we can see that he was not only adopting a wider range of artistic skills but that he was also seeking out the best teachers from whom he could acquire these new skills.

In 1899, at 35 years of age, Qi became a pupil of Wang Kaiyun, learning poetry and, at that time, published his first collection of seal-making exhibits that he named 'Ji Yuan Album of Seals'.

The following year, 1900, saw the start of a new century. Qi left his house that he had named 'Xingdoutang' and moved to another one he called 'Meigongci'. He applied the metaphor 'Jie shan yin guan', which has the meaning of his having borrowed the mountain to build this small house.

In 1902, at 38 years of age, Qi went to Xi'an in north-west China. This was the first time that he had ever left Xiangtan and while there he was introduced to Fan Fanshan, a collector of many authentic works of ancient artists and a man of literature. He was also an official in the Manchu Qing dynasty. This provided Qi with the inspiration to further enhance his artistic skills.

The following year, 1903, upon receiving an invitation from Xia Wuyi to go with him to Xi'an, Qi was offered the opportunity to become a royal painter for the Queen Mother, Ci Xi, having been introduced by Fan Fanshan, but, despite all efforts to get him to do otherwise, he insisted on rejecting the position. It is not known exactly why this was so but it was perhaps to avoid the dangerous political intrigues of the time. His attitude may perhaps be discerned from an early age. When Qi Baishi was 6 years old, there was a new official appointed in Xiangtan county. A big ceremony in the countryside was held to celebrate his inauguration and almost everybody went to watch it, except for Qi Baishi. His mother urged him to go but he said, "We feed ourselves by our own hands. There is no need to feel proud to be an official."

For eight restless years, from 1902 to 1909, Qi travelled extensively throughout China to places such as Xi'an, Beijing Tianjin, Han Kou, Jiangxi, Guangdong, Shanghai, and outside of (then) mainland China to Hong Kong. He also travelled to Vietnam. He left and then came back to Xiangtan some five times, and became acquainted with several cultural and literary people with whom he studied a lot of authentic works by ancient artists. In 1911, in middle age, he met Chen Shizeng, a famous academic at the time, in Beijing. Their meeting and the onset of their subsequent friendship is considered to be a major turning point in his career. In 1919, he married his second wife, Hu Baozhu, and finally settled down with her in Beijing.

In 1922, Chen Shizeng, whose pseudonyms are 'Hengque' and 'Xiu Daoren', and Kuitang, who was a famous artist and educator in China, took Qi's paintings to Japan, in order to display them at an exhibition in Tokyo. This event featured paintings by artists from China as well as those from Japan. Qi managed to sell all of his paintings. Two were subsequently selected for public display in Paris, France.

In 1927, Qi was invited by the Director of the Beijing Art Academy, Lin Fengmian, to teach traditional painting and, during the same year, was appointed a professor there. The following year, 1928, he published *Baishi Seal-making* and *Jie Shan Yin Guan Album of Poems*. Three years later, in 1931, he published *Baishi Poems*.

In 1937, the Sino-Japanese war started and China was invaded, with both Beijing and Tianjin, two major centres of the country, being occupied. Qi was 66 years of age at the time. He reacted by retiring from the world, shutting himself away and refusing to see anyone.

Qi also listened to the advice of the fortune teller that he went to see in Changsha. He was advised to add two years to his real age. This was regarded as being fortunate for him, although how so is not clear. Therefore, from then on, he declared himself to be two years older than his actual age. This age, of course, as previously explained, was already two years older than the modern Western calculation. This may seem counter-intuitive to any modern-day, age-conscious narcissists!

In 1940, his first wife, Chen Chunjun, died and he wrote a eulogy 'Ode to Mrs Chen' to remember her by. In 1944, his second wife, Hu Baozhu, also died. The long war with Japan finally ended in 1945. The ongoing Chinese Civil War was however still unfinished and this took on further momentum once fighting the Japanese ended. China was still racked by upheaval until 1949.

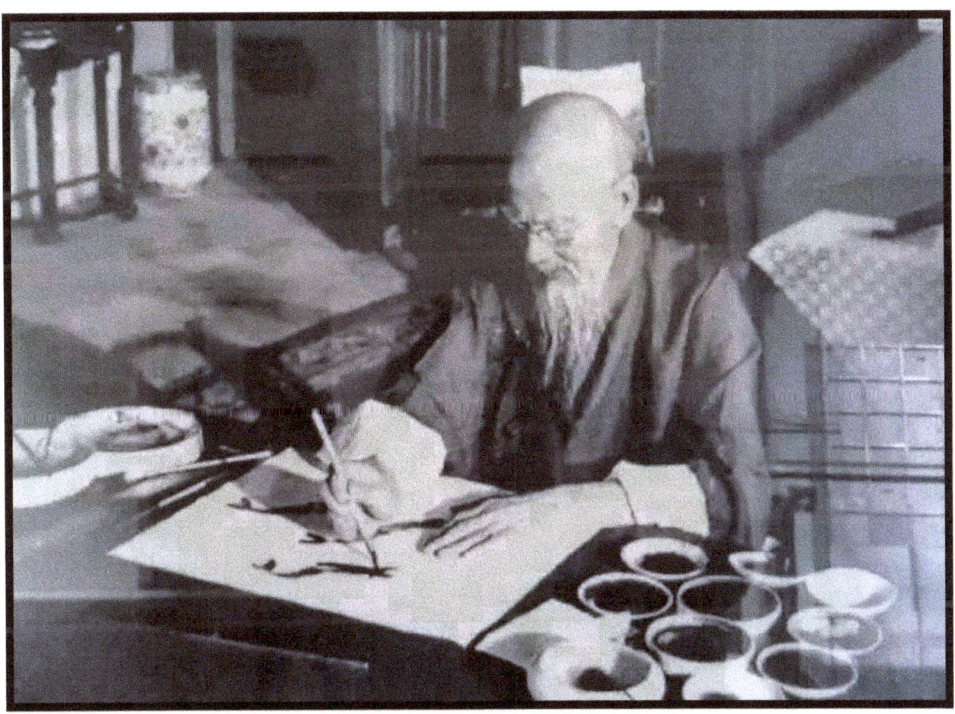

Image 1-4: Qi Baishi painting at his desk

In 1946, Qi continued to sell his works in Beijing. In October, he went to Nanjing and Shanghai to open his exhibitions. All his works were sold out but the financial sums he received as paper currency were not sufficient to be exchanged for even ten bags of flour. This was due to the extreme currency devaluation at that time.

In 1949, Qi was invited to meet President Zhou Enlai, and he brought with him two carved seals to present to Chairman Mao Zedong. These two people were the two most prominent members of the new Communist government. The following year, 1950, Qi became the Honorary Professor of the Central Academy of Fine Arts and a member of the Central Research Institute of Culture and History. During that winter and the following spring, his works were displayed in a charity exhibition called 'Resist-America, Aid Korea' in Beijing and Shenyang.

In 1952, Qi's huge, colourful painting named *Hundreds of Flowers and Doves of Peace* was dedicated to the Peace Committee of Asia and the Pacific Region. He painted many works about peace during that year.

By 1953 Qi was 89 years of age and almost at the end of his life, yet still was declaring himself to be even older than was necessary by the current age calculations, at 91 years! One wonders who the fortune teller was! More than two hundred cultural and literary people attended his announced birthday party, and the Ministry of Culture granted him the title of Outstanding Artist of the Chinese People. President Zhou Enlai attended his birthday dinner. In October, he was selected as the first president of the China Art Association.

The next year, 1954, Qi was selected as the representative of the Chinese people and then attended the first National Peoples' Congress. In July of the following year, 1955, he painted the great work *Song of Peace* with Chen Banding, He Xiangning and fourteen other artists, that was dedicated to the World Peace Congress. On 27 April 1956, he was awarded the World Peace Prize by the World Peace Council.

On 15 May 1957, Qi was appointed honorary chairman of the Beijing China Gallery. During May and June of that year, he completed his final painting: *Peony*. On 16 September of that year he died In Beijing, aged 93. Following his death, in 1963 he was awarded the title of being 'one of the ten greatest cultural celebrities of China'.

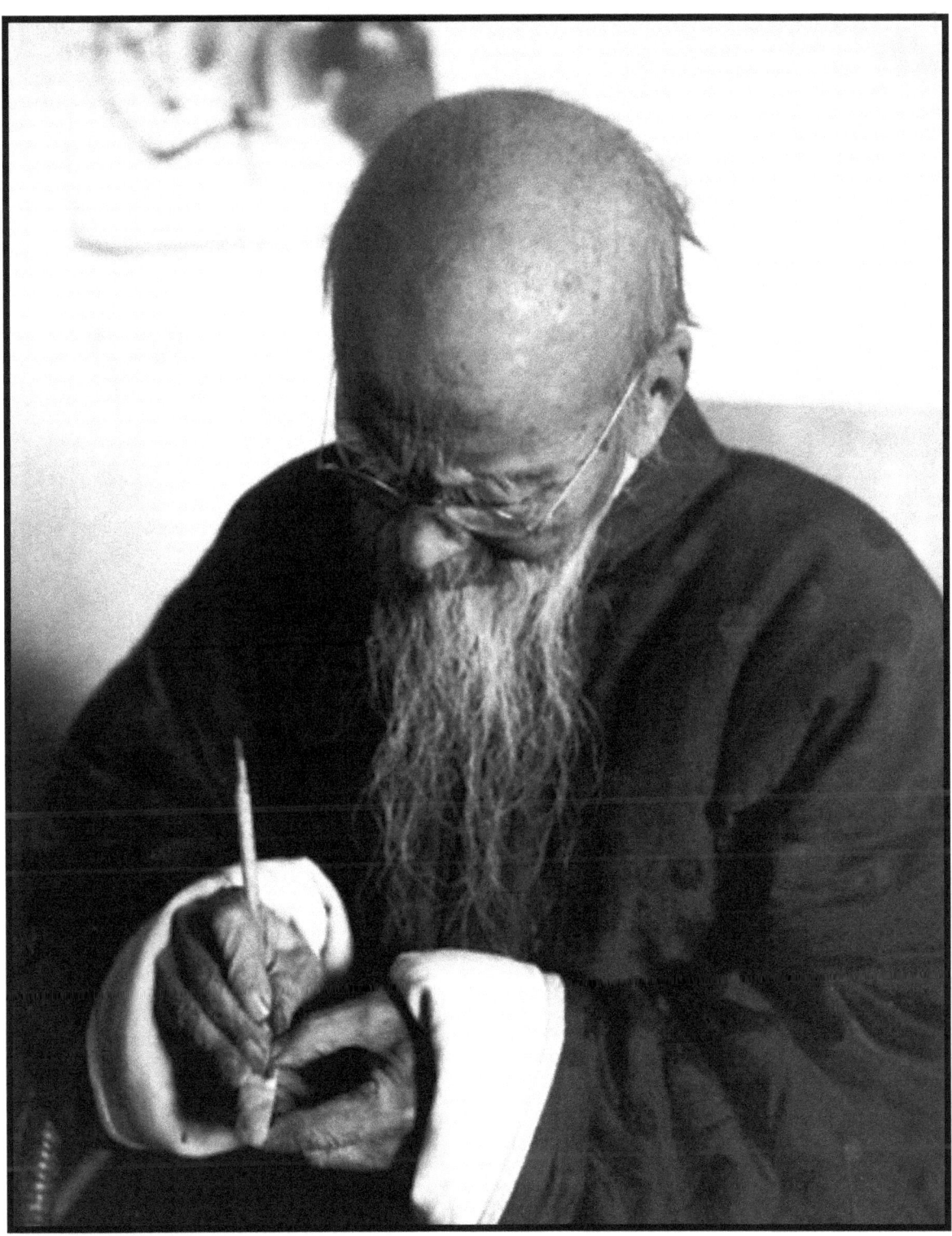

Image 1-5: Qi Baishi making a seal

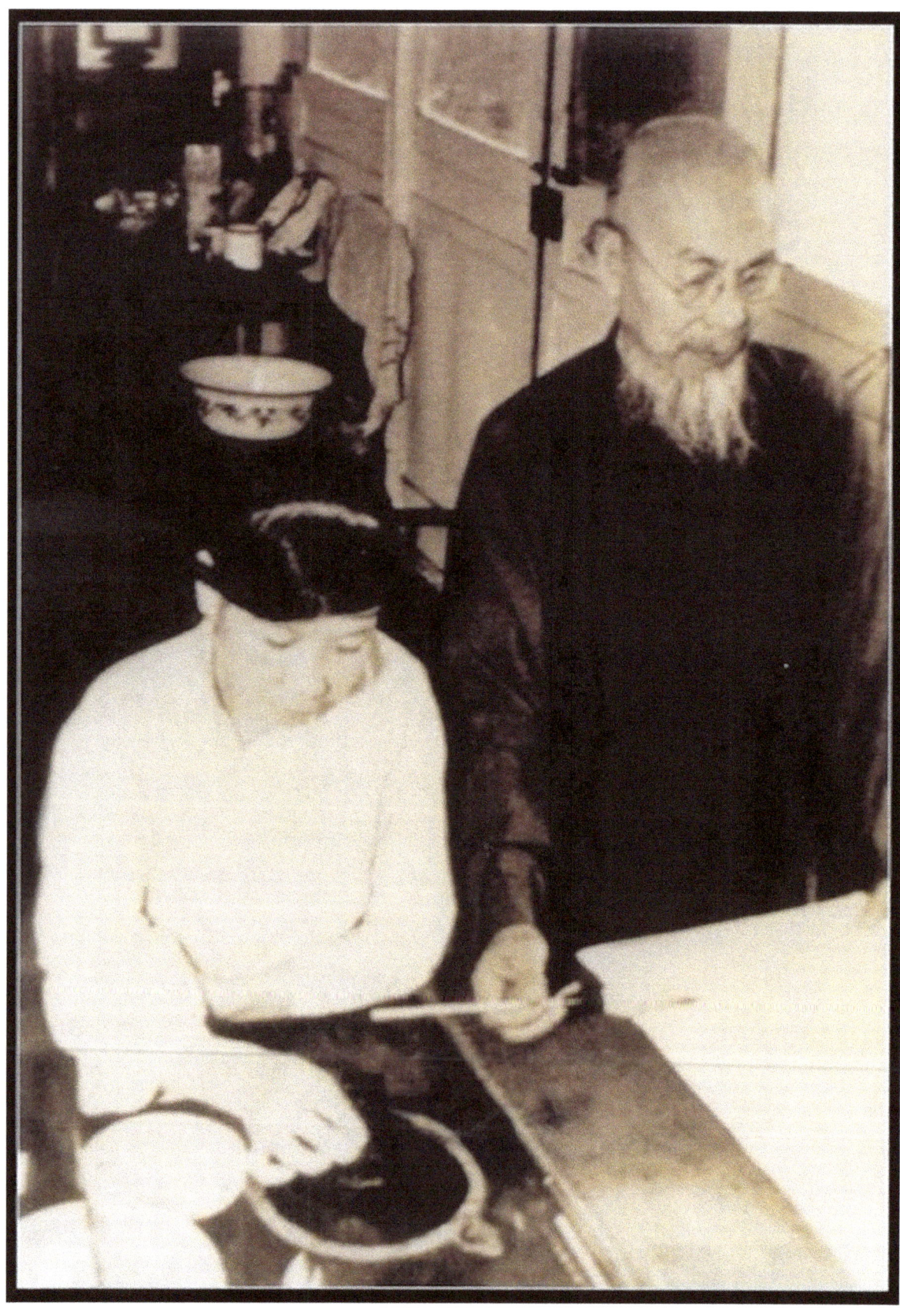

Image 1-6: Qi Baishi and his second wife, Hu Baozhu

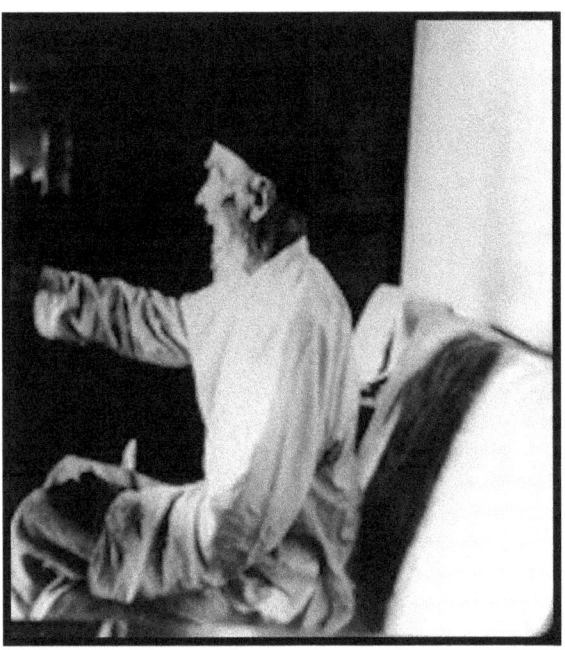

Image 1-7: Qi Baishi painting

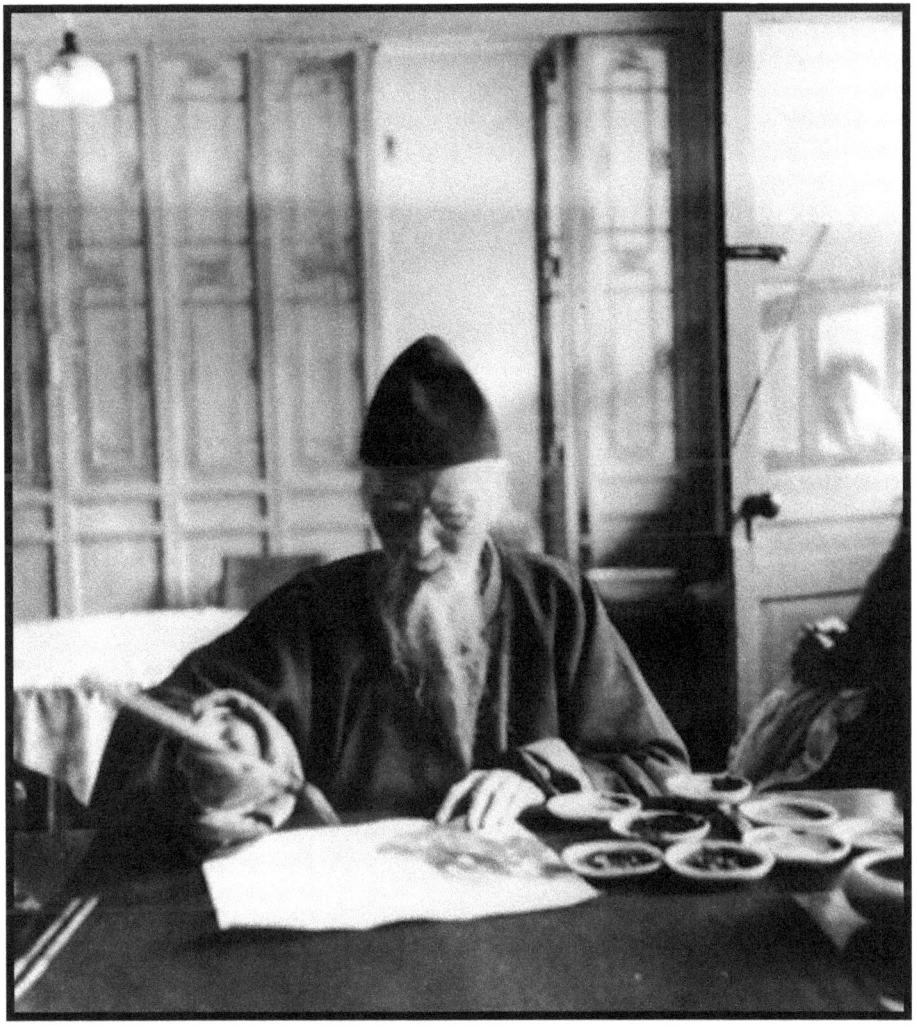

Image 1-8: Qi Baishi painting a shrimp

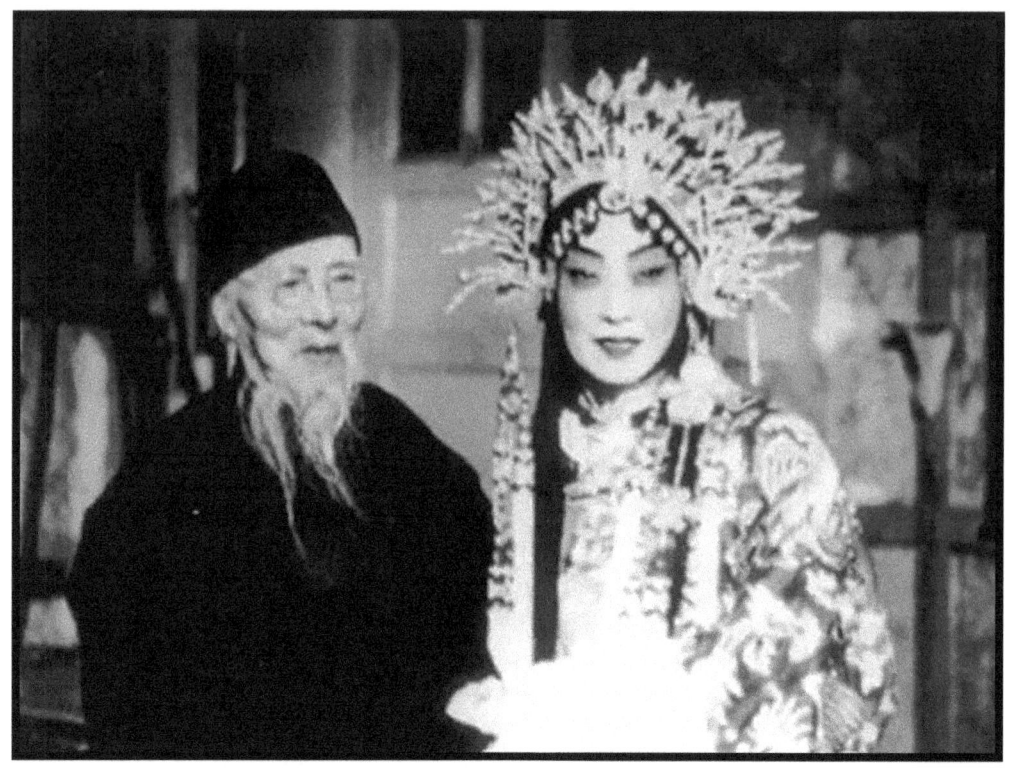

Image 1-9: Qi Baishi with Mei Lanfang, a Beijing opera star

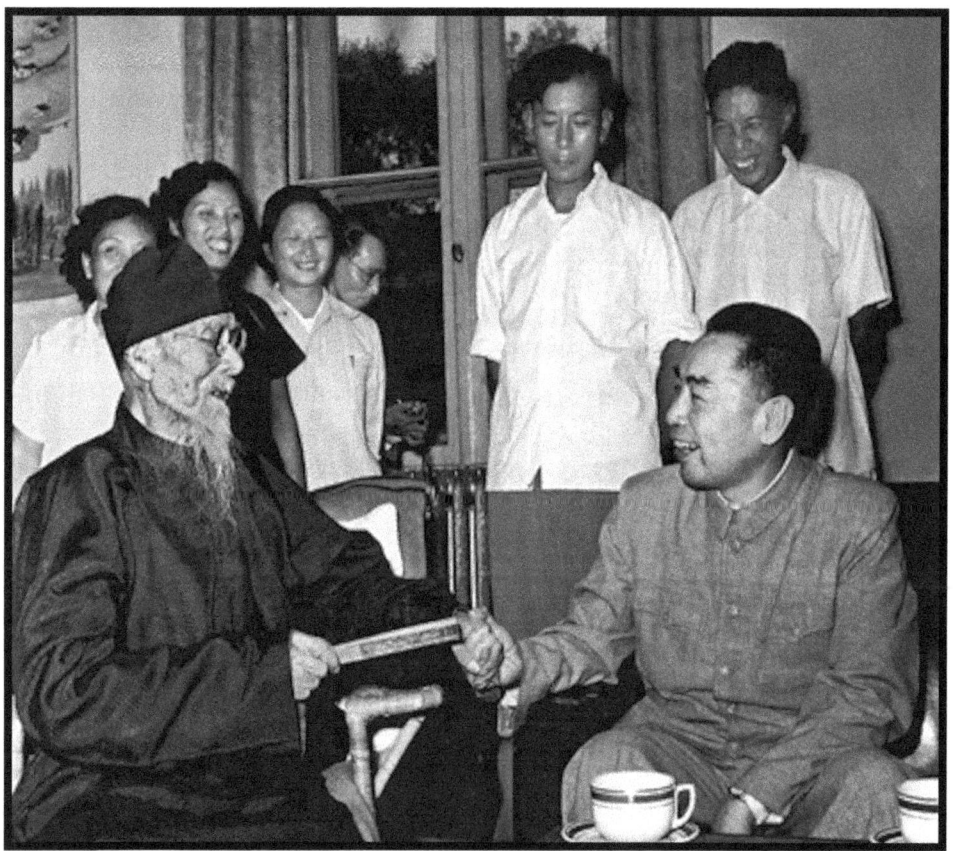

Image 1-10: Qi Baishi with Zhou Enlai, the Chinese President

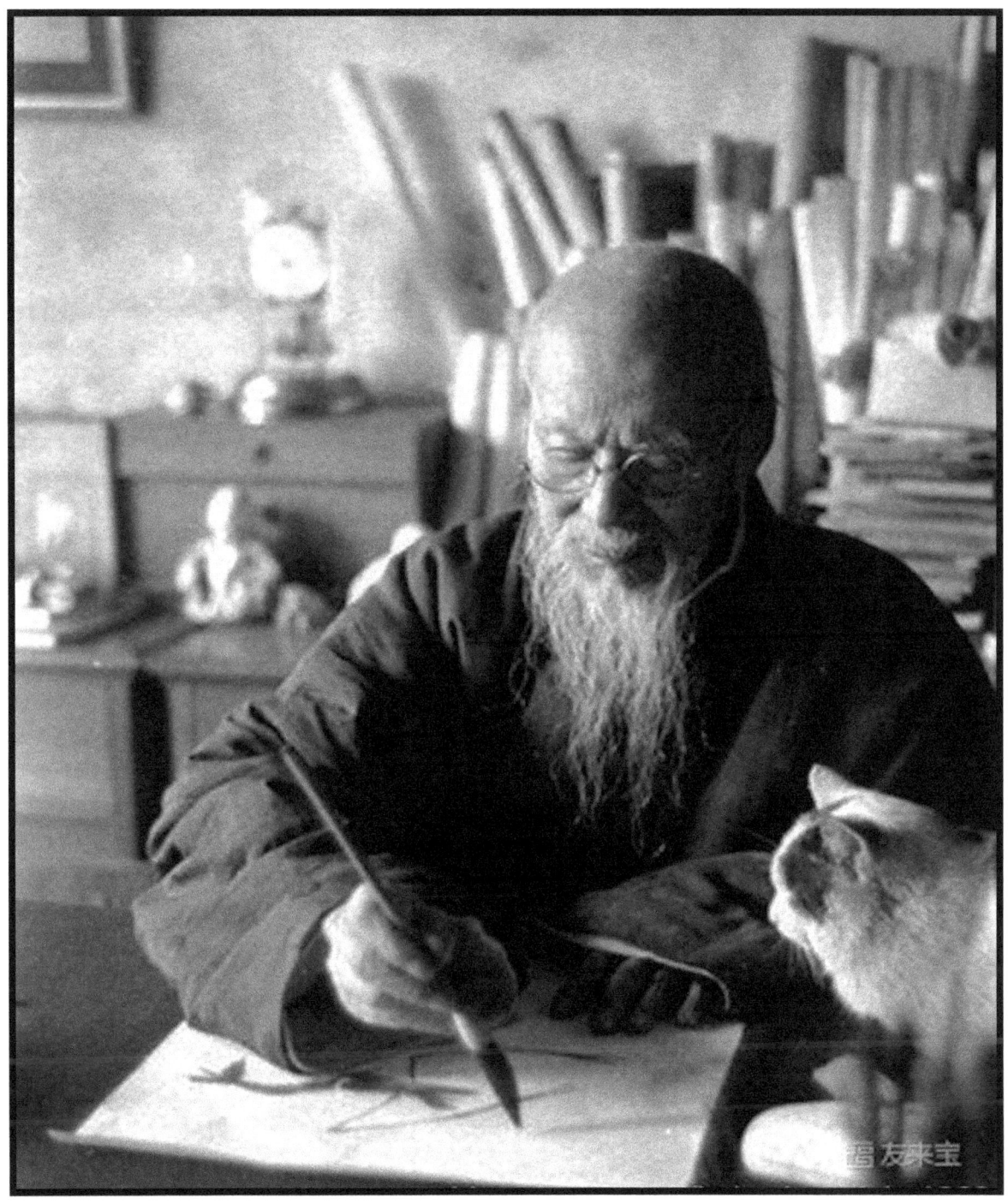

Image 1-11: Qi Baishi painting a shrimp

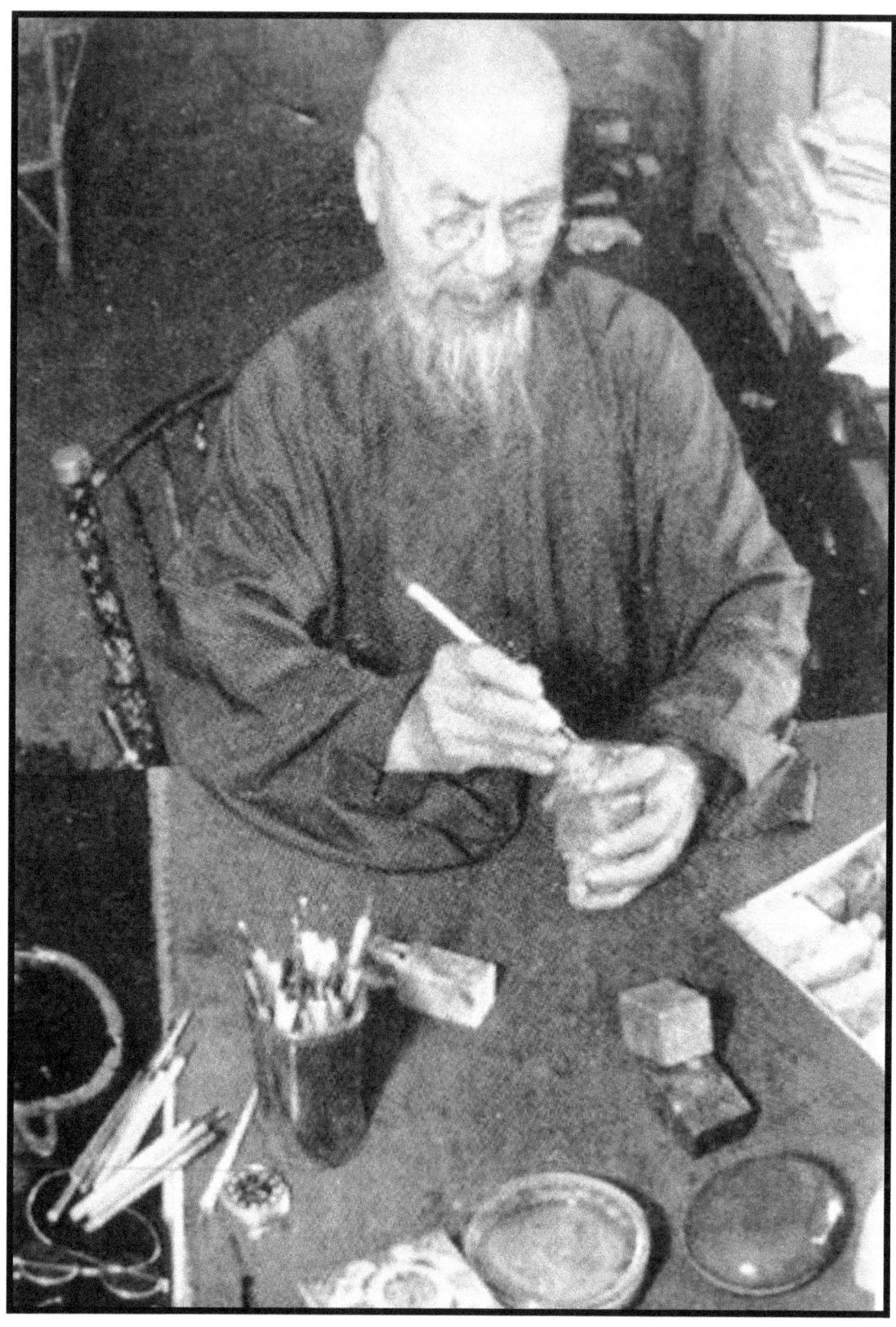

Image 1-12: Qi Baishi making a seal

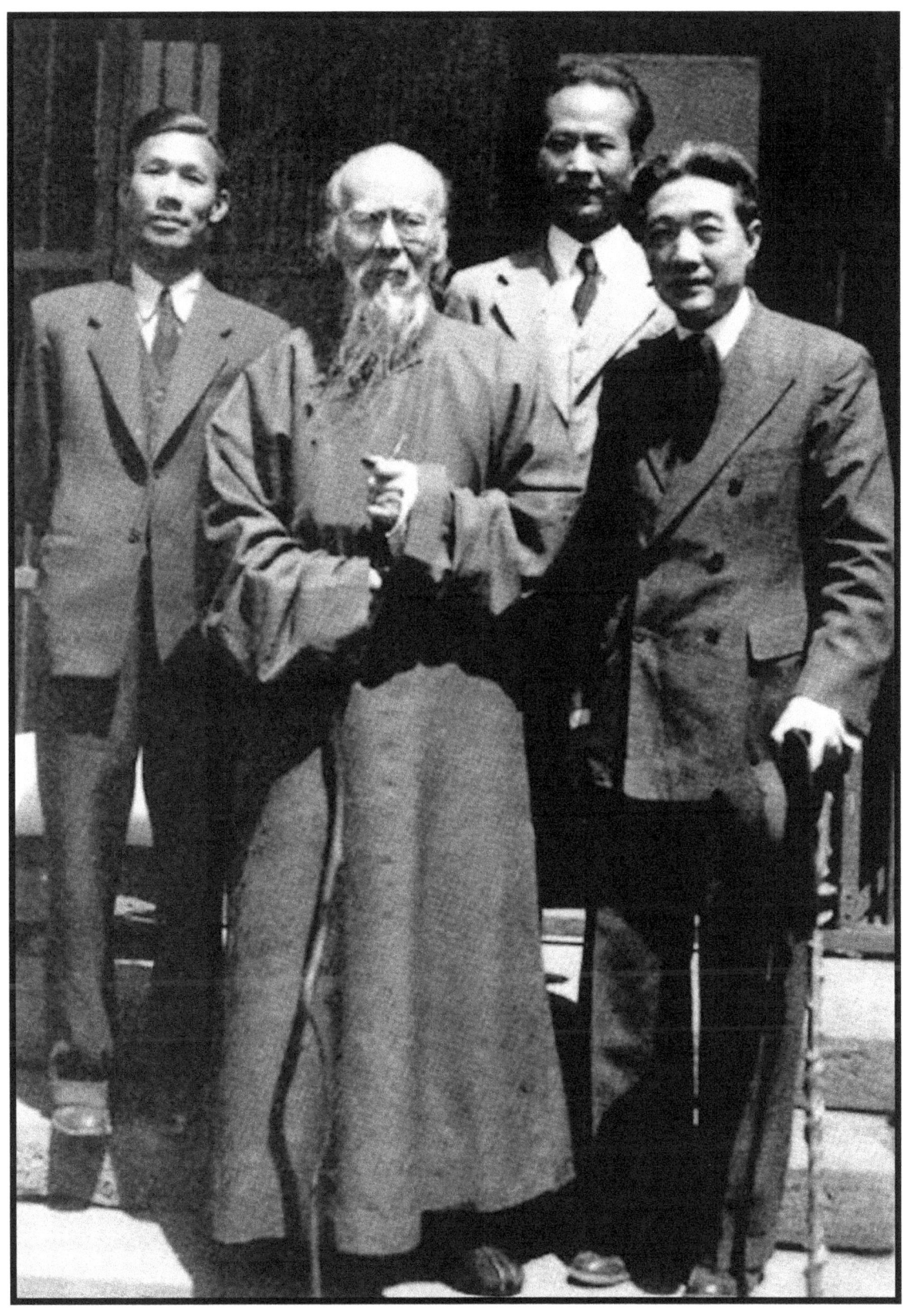

Image 1-13: Qi Baishi with famous artist Xu Beihong

Chapter Two: The Works of Qi Baishi 1

1. **Three Fish**

Type: Traditional Chinese water painting.

Qi Baishi: "I painted this picture for my brother Zipan and then my other brother Langxian also asked for one."

Signature: Baishi Shanweng Huang.

Read Seal: Baishi Weng.

Description:
From ancient times, Chinese artists have made use of poetry within their paintings and have therefore created a genre known as 'literary painting'. This type of painting not only demands great skill but also attests to the artist's level of skill and absorption of traditional Chinese culture. A truly classical Chinese painting therefore has four elements: a poem, calligraphy, drawing skill and seal-making.

The word for 'fish' in Chinese is pronounced 'yu', which is a homophone of 'left'. Fish symbolise wealth and luck, so there is a Chinese idiom 'Nian Nian You Yu', meaning 'abundance throughout the year'. During the San Guo dynasty, there was a man who taught his students that they should study hard always: in winter, at night and even when it was raining. Therefore these three conditions are known as 'San Yu'.

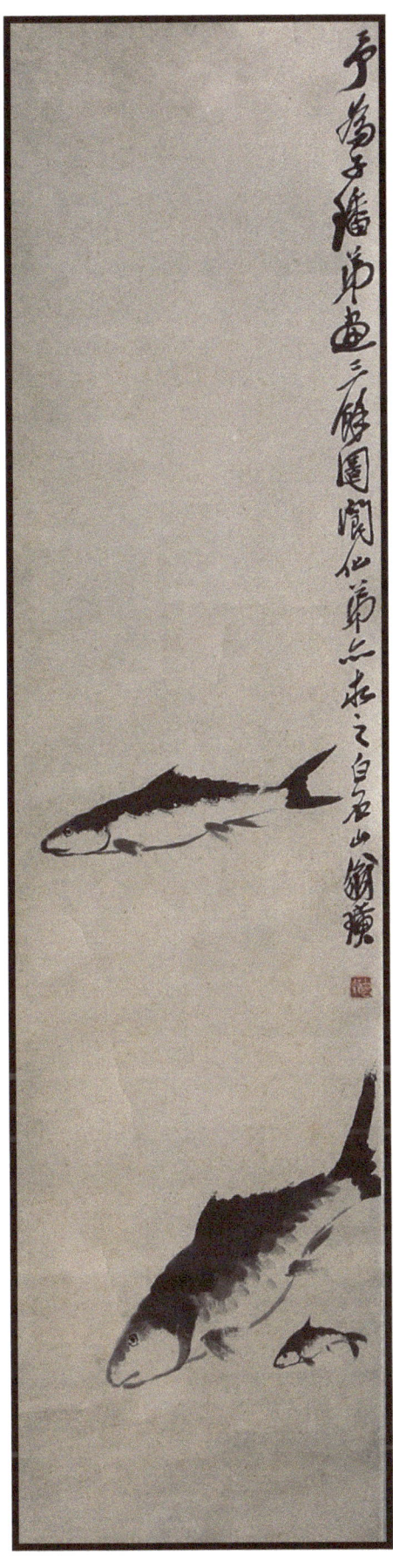

Image 2-1: Three Fish

2. Lychee and Squirrel

Type: Traditional Chinese water painting.

Signature: Xing Jiwu Laomin Qi Da (Qi's pseudonym) when he was living as a guest in Beijing. He was 90 years of age.

Read Seal: Jie Shanweng (Qi's pseudonym)

Description:

The lychee is a sweet fruit. Literary people and artists are said to love it. Many of them have created their artistic works around it as the subject. During the Tang dynasty, there was a story told about the lychee and many ancient stories were told about it throughout China. In one, the Tang Emperor Minghuang had a concubine whose name was Yang Guifei. She loved to eat lychee. At that time, however, the lychee only grew in the south of the country. So, Tang Minghuang built a road so that his soldiers could transport the lychee. He was very fond of the concubine and wanted to make her happy.

The Chinese pinyin word for lychee is 'lizhi'. The 'li' part of lizhi is a homophone of 'lucky'. Qi loved to draw lychee and loved to eat the lychee of Qinzhou. It looks as though the squirrel he has painted also likes to eat lychee. It wants to eat it but is afraid that it may fall off the tree, so it fastens on tightly to the tree trunk. The tree trunk is drawn using light ink to highlight the difference in colour with the squirrel and to make it look more open and transparent.

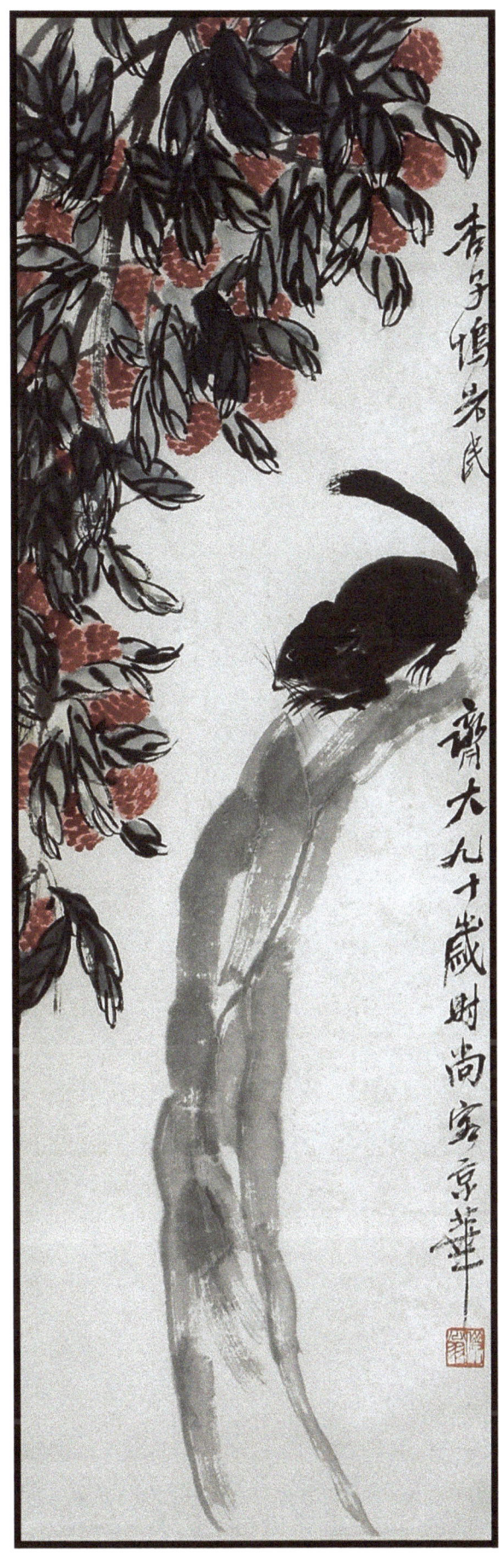

Image 2-2: Lychee and Squirrel

3. Cockscomb and Chicks

Type: Traditional Chinese water painting.

Signature: Jiao Zi Jia Guan. Jie Shan Lao Ren (Qi' pseudonym) when he was living as a guest in Beijing aged of 86.

Read Seal: Qi Da (Qi's pseudonym). Lu Ban Men Xia (Qi's pseudonym).

Description:

'Jiao zi jia guan' is an idiom in China that means 'hoping one's children will have a bright future'. The big cockerel and five chicks are gathered together. It looks as though the cockerel is teaching his chicks something. There is a red cockscomb stretching from outside of the painting, just at the top of the picture, and this looks very striking. The word 'teach' in Chinese is pronounced 'jiao'. Chicks are the children of the cockerel so they are 'zi'. The word 'cockscomb' in Chinese is pronounced 'ji guan hua', so using the word 'guan' and combining the words together makes them into an idiom in Chinese. This is 'jiao zi jia guan'.

The picture depicts the harmony and auspiciousness. Besides this, the cockerel looks very perky, and each chick has a different manner. None of them looks the same. They seem to be listening carefully to their father and even thinking deeply. The different strengths of ink and water used make the painting look as though it has different colours. This skill is very advanced and the arrangement of the whole painting is superb.

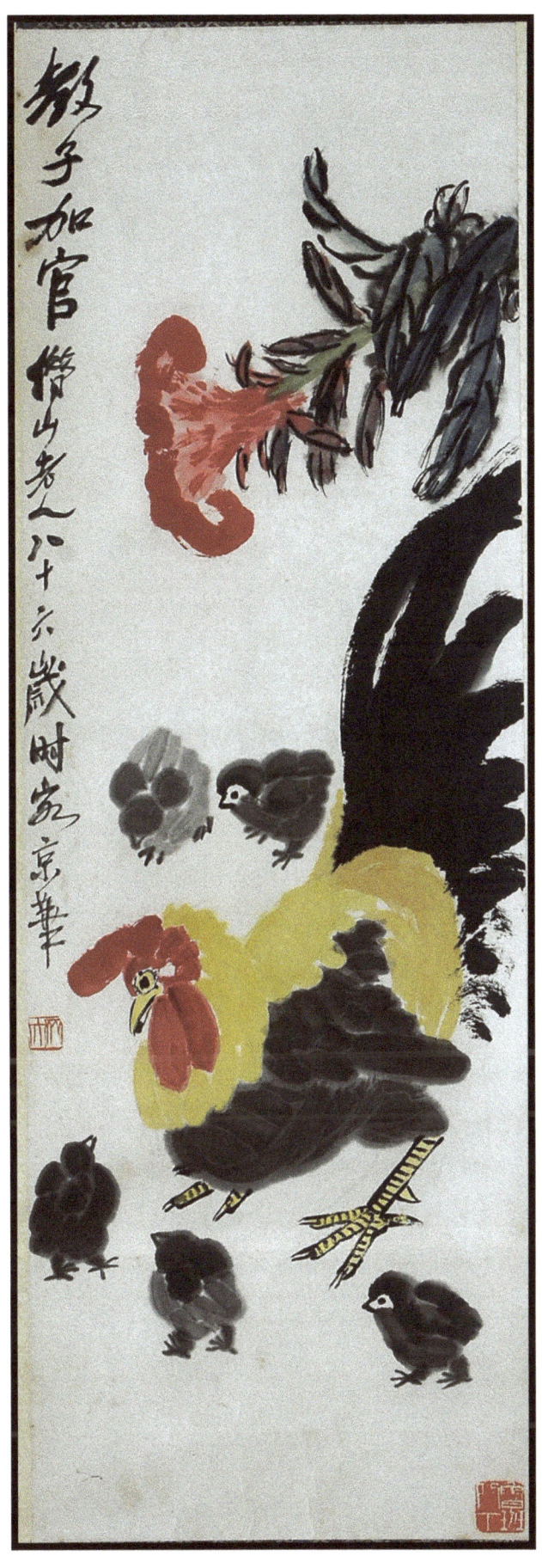

Image 2-3: Cockscomb and Chicks

4. Begonias

Type: Traditional Chinese water painting.

Read Seal: Mu Jushi (Qi's pseudonym).

Qi Basihi: "The original begonia was depicted as growing on the ground at a level of about 2 chi. There were no leaves on it. This one was an artificial begonia, which was created by Zhao Weishu. Artists are able to apply their imagination in their paintings. I didn't paint this type very often."

Description:
The two begonias have grown tall and there is great variety in the depth of colour. The Chinese believe that an ink and water combination can produce different colours, so the leaves look different with the swirling effect of colours. Some of them are in front while others are beneath, creating a natural and changeable look. It looks as though there is a wind blowing the flowers and leaves, making them appear to be moving.

This is a countryside symphony; a life song. The calligraphy on the painting explains that this kind of begonia is a creation by Zhao Weishu, who was a Chinese artist during the Qing dynasty, and that it is not a real begonia. It proves that Qi Baishi respected nature and made his sketches from life. He gave this explanation in order to present his perspectives to the audience.

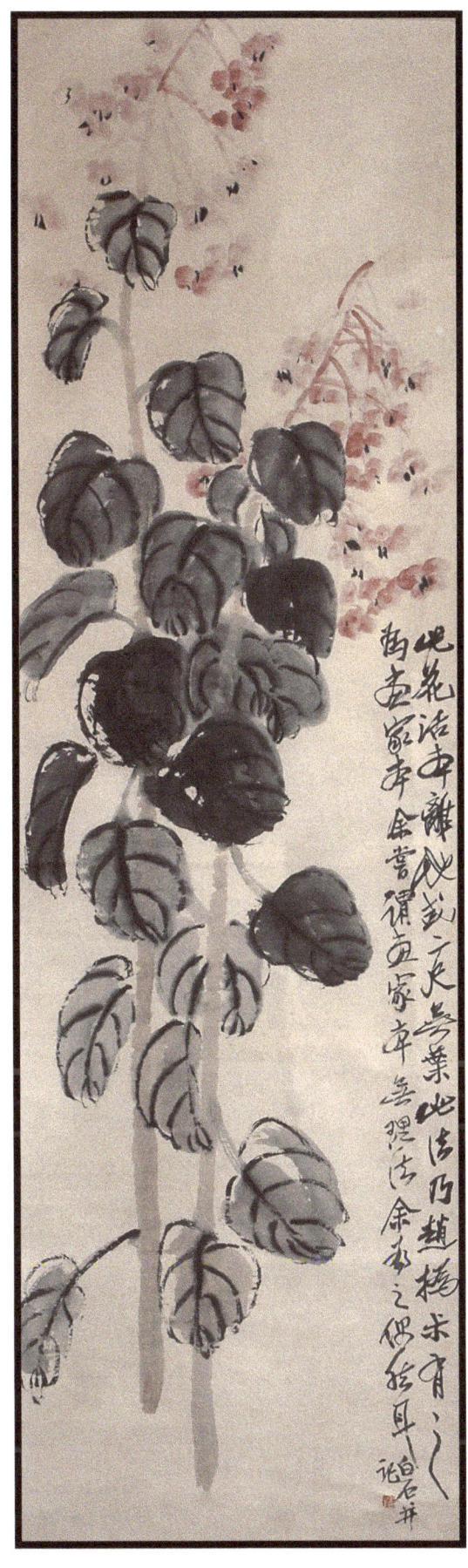

Image 2-4: Begonias

5. Cabbage and Grasshopper

Type: Traditional Chinese water painting.

Inscription: Qi Baishi wrote on the picture: "In the early of Jia Xu age, in October, the weather isn't cold and I can paint freely. When I am painting this picture for my female student Xiurong, about twenty students are watching."

Read Seal: Baishi.

Description:

Qi Baishi's favourite vegetable was the cabbage. There are three cabbages in this picture and they look very fresh as though they have just been dug out of the earth. Qi used different combinations of ink and water to make each cabbage look different. The leaves curl naturally, which makes them look real. We can almost smell the fragrance from those sweet cabbages.

The grasshopper is vibrant and looks as though it has just jumped out from the cabbages, because its perspective is seemingly from another direction. This picture combines movement and stillness together, making the picture look animated.

Someone once asked Qi, "How could you draw the cabbages so superbly?" Qi answered, "You aren't a farmer, so you would just draw the shape but not capture the spirit." This is entirely the point. Qi was born into a farming family and so was used to seeing these objects on a daily basis. Only when you know someone or something well are you able to capture the characters and emotions.

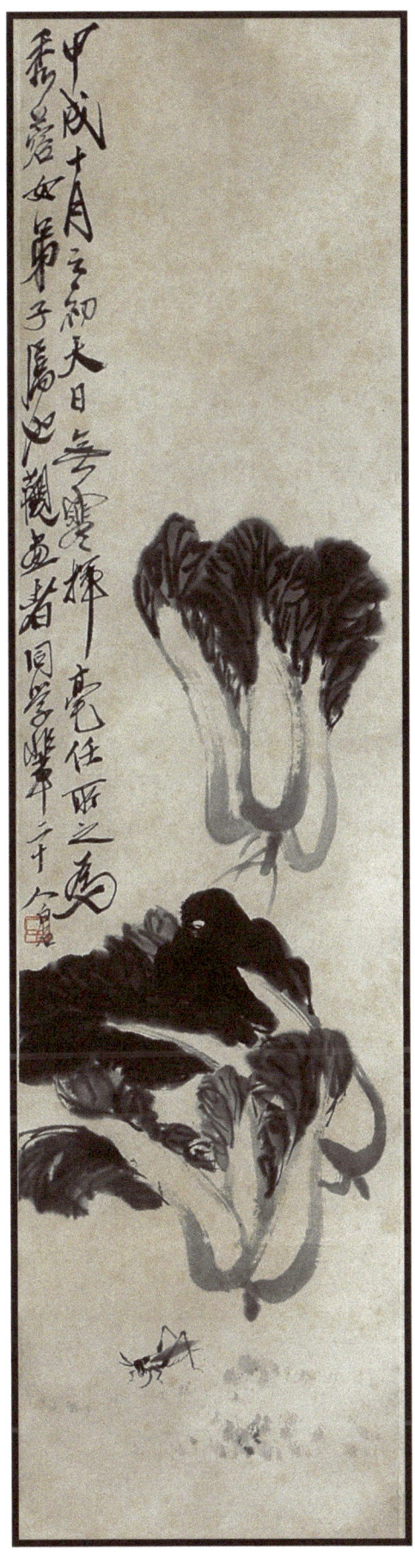

Image 2-5: Cabbage and Grasshopper

6. Fortunate Mandarin Ducks

Type: Traditional Chinese water painting.

Inscription: Ji Ping old man Baishi inscribed: Fortunate Mandarin Duck.

Read Seal: Qi Da (Qi' pseudonym).

Description:

The lotus is covered by leaves and is slim and graceful. The leaves are very pliable and moist. Their black colour strongly contrasts with the red lotus, making you see the delicacy and charm of the flower. The mandarin ducks are swimming about under the leaves; one of them is turning its head back to look at the leaves. This pair of mandarin ducks is colourful and full of child-like innocence, which represents pure love and a harmonious family. The lotus represents peace and happiness, and Qi wrote 'Fu lv Yuan Yang' – a very lucky and fortunate and loving bird, implying fortune and harmony. The ducks are known as mandarin ducks in English.

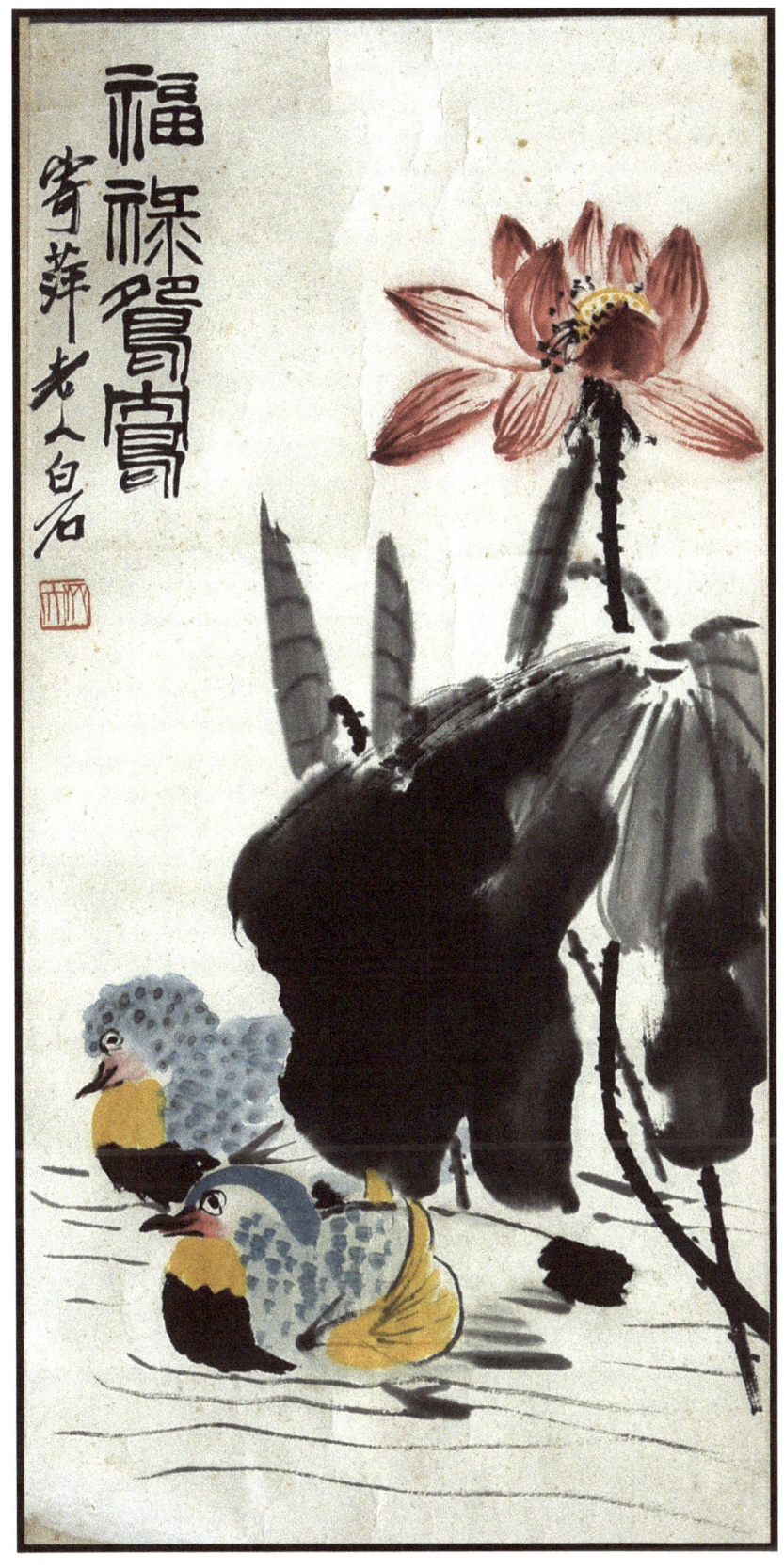

Image 2-6: Fortunate Mandarin Ducks

7. Yanlaihong (Young Old Man) and Dragonfly

Inscription: My wife Baozhu requested this painting for Mrs Xishang.

Read Seal: Lao Bai - Baishi Huachong (Qi's pseudonym).

Description:

The English translation of 'Yanlaihong' is 'young old man'. This is a traditional plant in China. Artists of the Qing dynasty who painted this kind of plant used watery colours and a gentle touch. This produced a refined look. Qi Baishi painted this Yanlaihong using strong red colours, which creates a happy, lucky feeling.

The leaves in the painting look different, with deep, swirling colours. Some of them are placed in the foreground while others sit beneath them, looking natural and changeable. Qi painted this while expressing his best wishes to Mrs Xishang and recognising his wish to be a young man. The painting showed Qi's confidence in himself and his hopes for his future life.

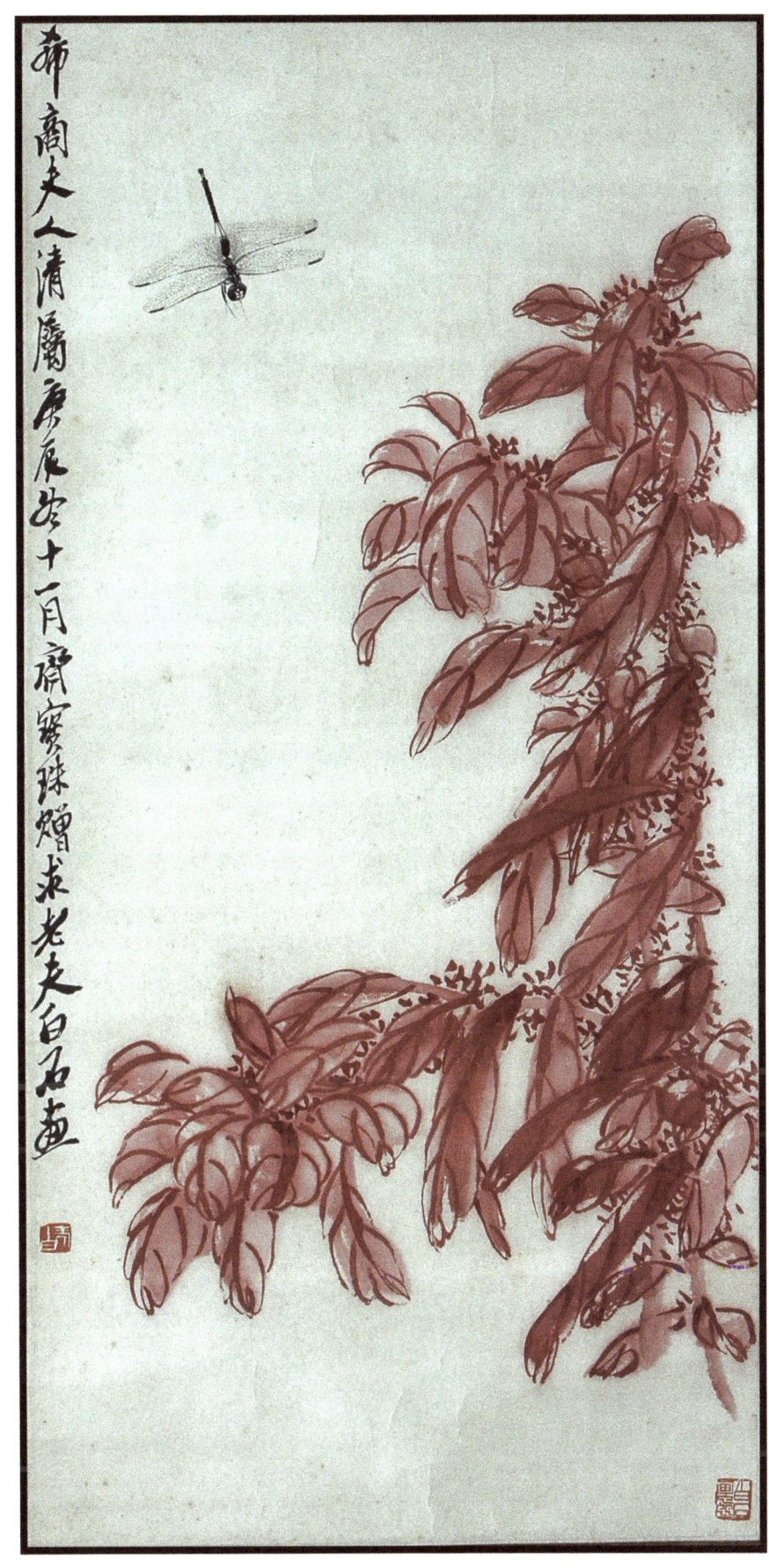

Image 2-7: Yanlaihong (Young Old Man) and Dragonfly

8. Chrysanthemum and Two Birds

Inscription: Baishi Shangweng wrote: "The empty space of this picture is not much, and although my friend asked me to write some poetry on it, I could not satisfy him."

Read Seal: Mu Jushi (Qi's pseudonym).

Description:

This picture is very 'busy'. It must have been hard to paint it this way but Qi made it look ethereal. He used freehand for this.

The middle line of the picture is the symmetry line. Also in the middle of the picture is a stone, which has two peaks. Two birds are standing on the peaks. Their countenance differs: one is staring at the other while the other is closing its eyes. Next to the larger peak there is a bunch of red yan laihong flowers, which are sited lower than the chrysanthemum.

The bird on the middle line looks very striking but is still harmonious with the surroundings. The control of pen and ink, colour and object are just right. At the top left of the painting, Qi wrote the reason why he couldn't write any poetry on it. The colour of the inscription matches the stone and the birds.

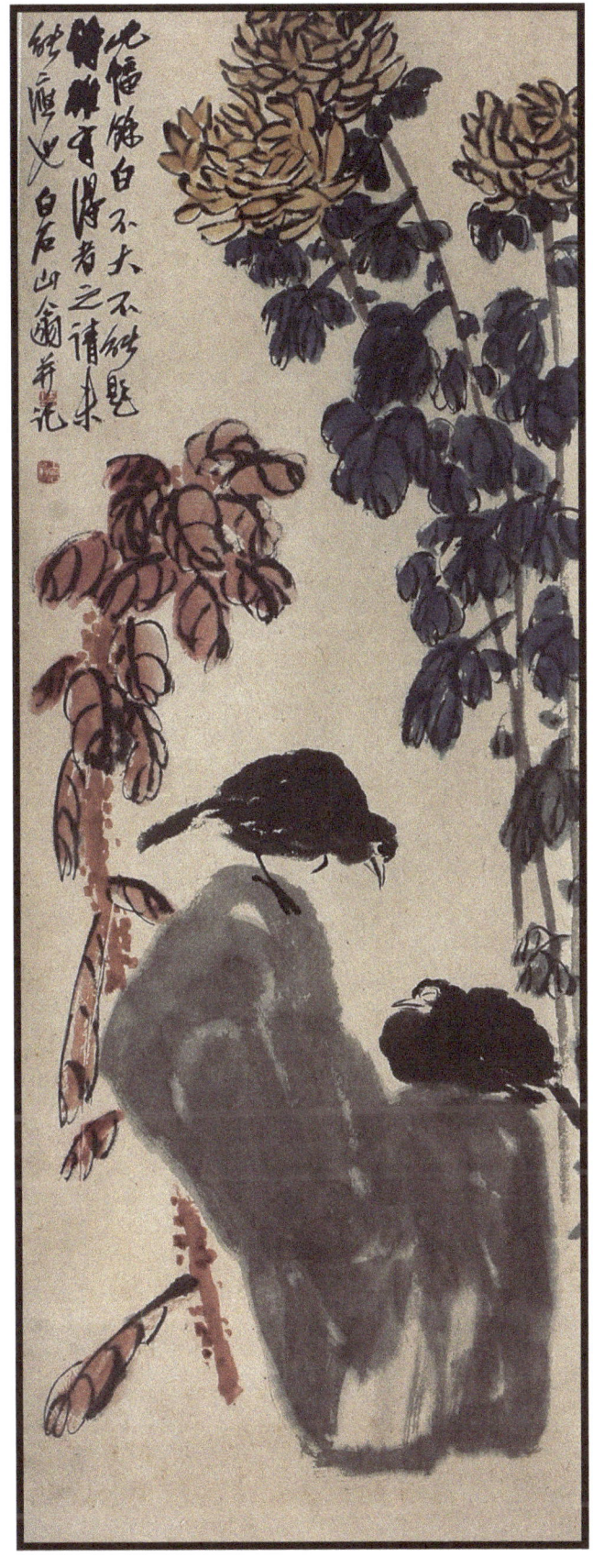

Image 2-8: Chrysanthemum and Two Birds

9. Shrimp 1

Inscription: The host of Jie Shan Yin Guan. "In the winter of Donghai, I am 87 years old and am a guest in Beijing."

Read Seal: Lao Mu (Qi's' pseudonym). Baishi.

Description:

Qi Baishi stated: "For so many years I have been painting shrimp and now finally I get their spirit."

We can imagine how hard it is for an artist to grasp the spirit of the shrimp. Before he was 58 years old, Qi was imitating the artists Ba Dashanren, Li Futang and Zheng Banqiao. The shape was 'just so' and hardly changed. From the age of 60, Qi began to change his style and, until he was 64 years old, he was sophisticated and flexible in his approach. Finally, he developed his own style and captured the character of the shrimp. He summarised it thus: "I have been painting shrimp for so many years and have changed my approach a lot. From the first change, they just looked like the real ones. From the second change, they were almost exactly like the real ones. From the third change, they were different in colour." Therefore, there were three changes in his painting of shrimp.

This picture is a classic shrimp painting. The shape, the use of pen and ink and the spirit applied are all totally 'free'. At one level, they are a group of shrimp. Individually, however, they are 'here, there and every where', looking aloof. Some are swimming as can been seen in the movement of the claws; some look as though they are whispering. There is a dreamlike world within the pond, which is vibrant and free.

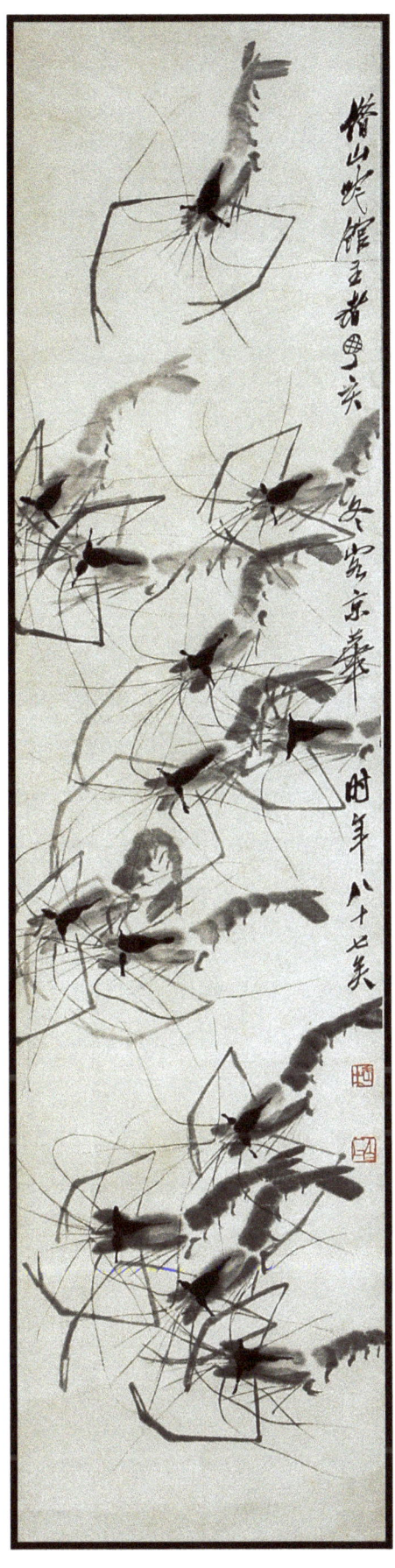

Image 2-9: Shrimp 1

10.   Shrimp 2

Inscription: Jie Shan Yin Guan Qi Huang.

Qi Huang wrote: "Please give me some advice, Mr Yuezhi."

This picture was painted in the summer of Jiaxu.

Read Seal: Lao Mu (Qi's pseudonym).

Description:

This painting was produced in 1934 when Qi was 70 years old. It represents the culmination of the three developments in Qi's painting of the shrimp. After the age of 64 years, he had been sophisticated and flexible. However, he still observed the shrimp carefully and imitated the works of other artists and altered his paintings repeatedly.

Adopting the philosophy that you must work hard and never give up during your whole life, this is the key as to how Qi refined his skills and became a success. He said, "The shrimp that I painted were different from the real ones we see. What I pursued is the spirit and not just the shape. So, the shrimp I painted are vivid and animated." This statement can help us to understand the beauty of Qi's painting.

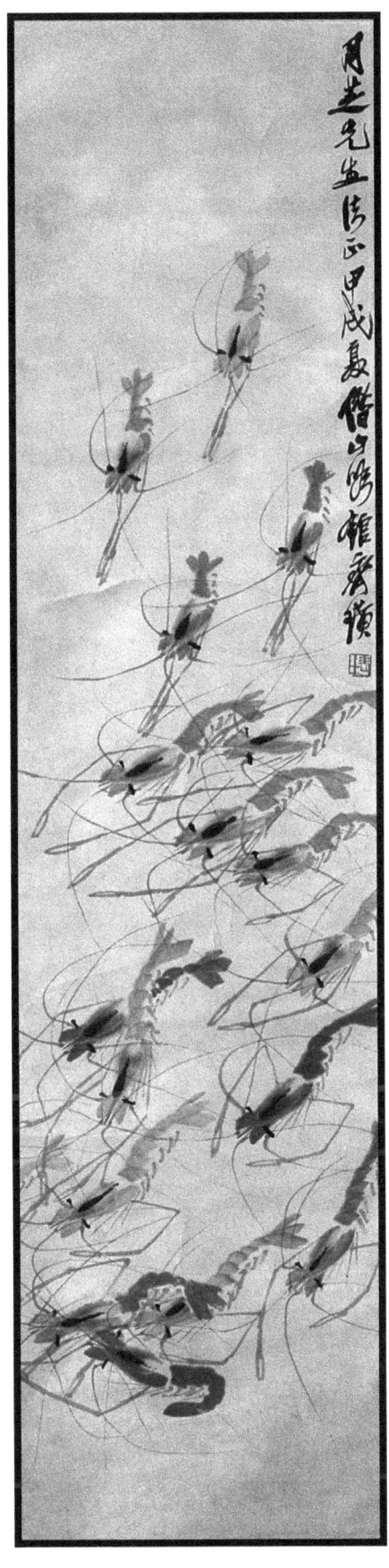

Image 2-10: Shrimp 2

11. Cushaws

Inscription: Until the 504 Jiazi year Ji Ping, old man Qi Baishi had lived in Beijing for 29 years.

Read seal: Qi Baishi.

Description:

Qi had previously been a farmer, so he was well acquainted with vegetables, flowers, birds and insects. Therefore, he was not only accomplished at painting small flowers and birds but also big vegetables. He adopted a refined and precise approach when he was painting the former and was generous and open with the latter.

Artists always drew cushaws in horizontally but Qi painted them vertically and gave them a totally smooth depiction. The vines are painted as sophisticated and twisted and the leaves are painted to look moist and dense. The cushaws were sketched with the ink lines on them looking heavier and stronger. The use of colour made the picture more interesting.

The direction of the cushaws, leaves and vines differs. The thickness of the ink is also varied. The light ink used for the vines makes the picture look vibrant and 'active' and this can be contrasted with the heavy ink leaves and vines. This makes the picture more distinguishable and contrasting.

Without the unique designs and superb control from Qi the picture would be very flat and dull. The subject matter was simple but the overall effect is of abundance. This shows what a talented artist Qi was.

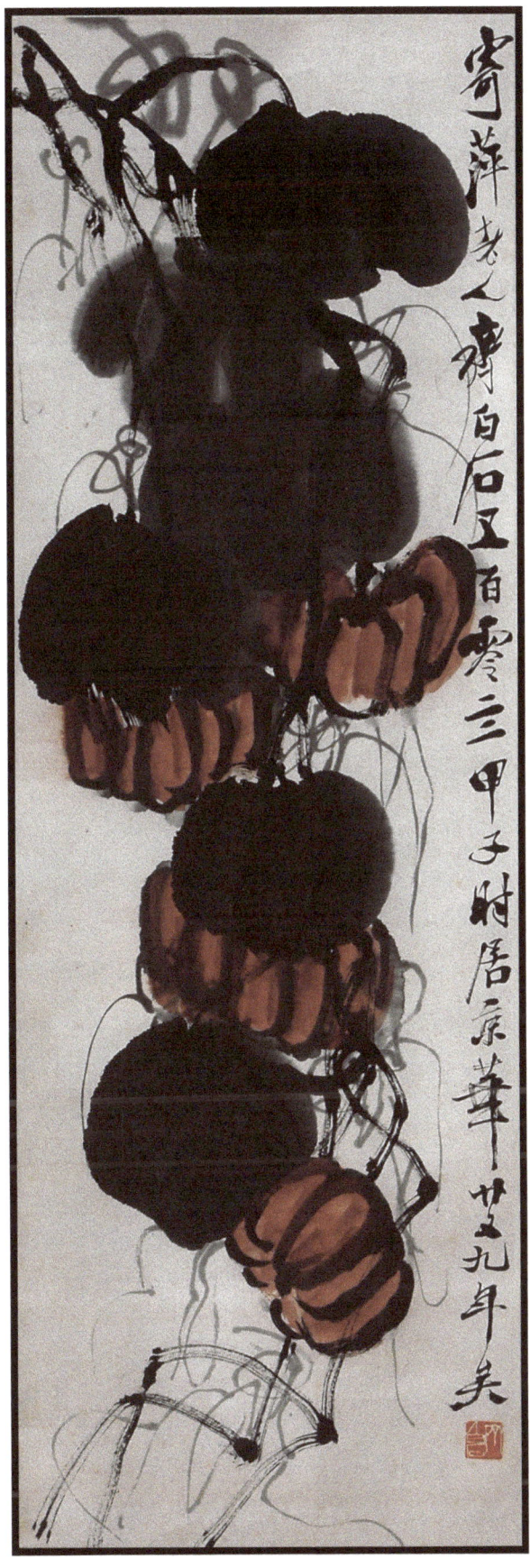

Image 2-11: Cushaws

12. Peaches, Pomegranates and Dragonfly

Inscription: 88-year-old Baishi wrote on the first of the Shuzi year: "I wish all elders to have longevity, and for youth have to have many children. My nephew Mr Xiang please have a long life."

Read Seal: Jie Shanweng (Qi's pseudonym), Baishi, I am an ordinary person. Longevity.

Description:

This is a thoughtful work that was requested by Qi's nephew in 1948. Several peaches and pomegranates stretch from the right-hand side into the picture. The branch is twisted, sophisticated and vibrant. The peach is striking and is painted alongside three different shaped pomegranates. One of the pomegranates looks very ripe as if the seeds are going to break out from the fruit. There is a dragonfly flying in towards the fruit, and this is painted in tiny detail.

The significance of the picture is that of sending a beautiful wish to others. The peach symbolises longevity, and the pomegranate holds many seeds and so the image is used to convey the idea of a couple having many offspring. The red seal states: "I am an ordinary person" and "longevity", which describes both Qi's homesickness and friendship.

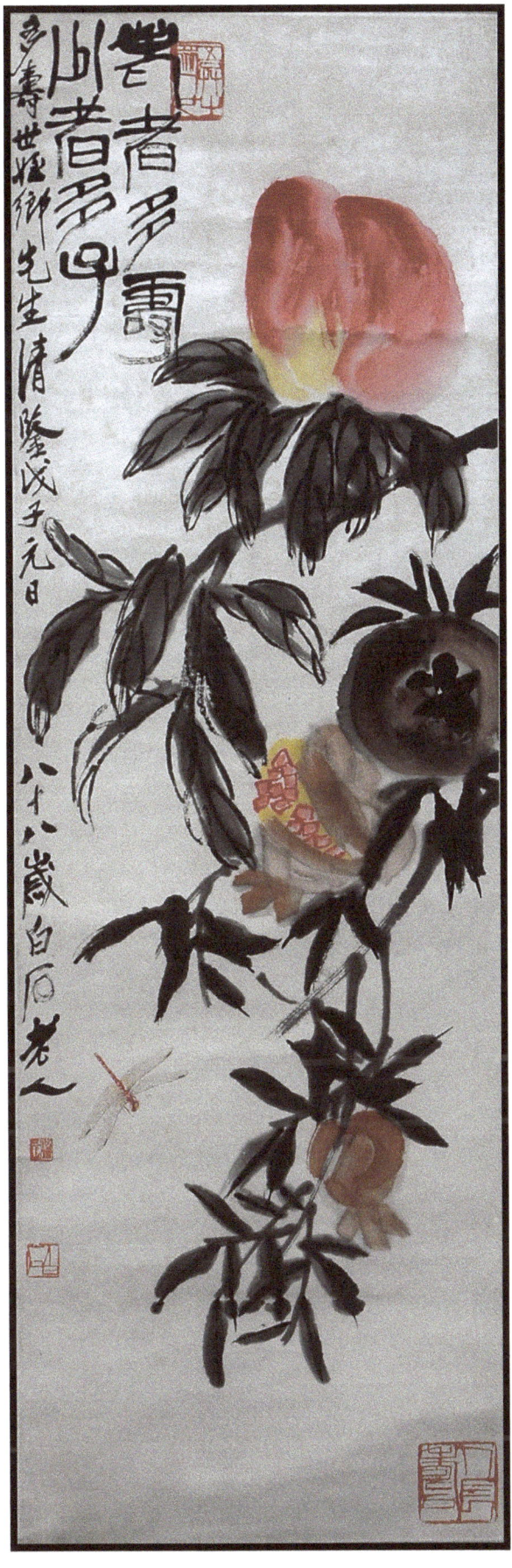

Image 2-12: Peaches, Pomegranates and Dragonfly

13. Lychee

Inscription: Baishi painted this at 82 years of age.

Read Seal: Qida.

Description:

Lychees grow in the south of China and are called by the Chinese 'the king of pomegranates'. They are sweet to eat and are loved by many people. The fruit is red and the leaves are green. This forms a sharp contrast in the painting. The word 'lychee' in Chinese is a homophone of 'lucky'. Therefore, the colour and the significance make the viewer feel that it is important and auspicious. This is the reason why artists always love to draw them. Qi drew lychees a lot. He went to Qizhou three times, eating some tasty lychees there and wrote poems and painted. Some of Qi's lychees were painted dangling and some were placed in a basket, with different designs and expressions. This painting was produced in 1942.

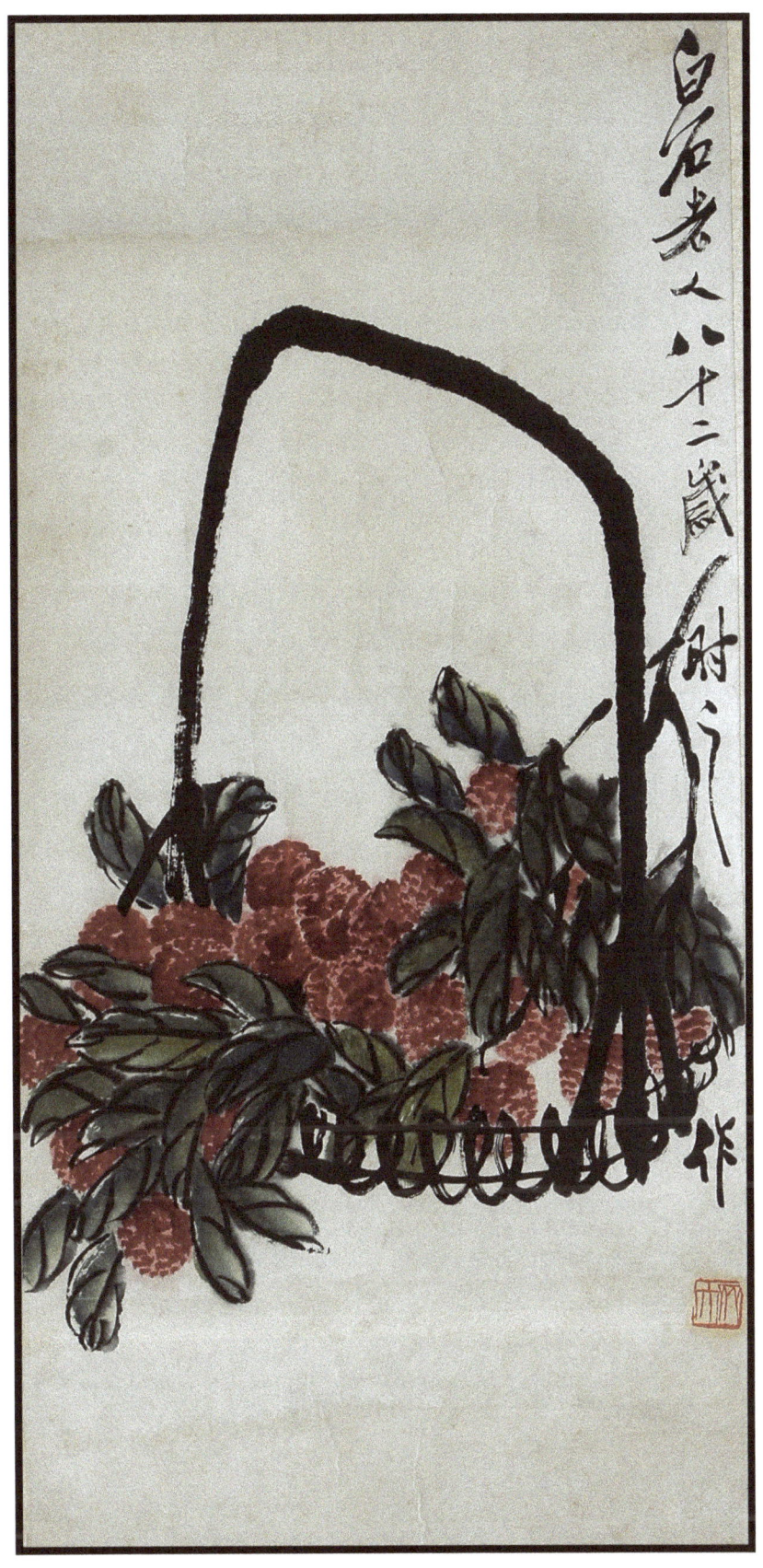

Image 2-13: Lychee

14. Lotus

Inscription: 88-year-old Baishi. Wuzi.

Read Seal: Baishiweng.

Description:
Qi Baishi was born in Xiangtan county in 1864 in an ordinary farmhouse. At the front of the house there was a pond called 'Star Pond'. In summer, many lotus blossomed in the pond. These were fragrant and symbolic of innocence and purity. This is the symbolism used for much Chinese Buddhist and Daoist imagery.

After Qi settled in Beijing, the lotus became one of the symbols he used to express his feeling of homesickness. After first arriving in Beijing, he felt very depressed because the people there initially didn't like his painting style and it was hard to sell his work. So, he changed his style to a more open and colourful one and the lotus became his signature work: red flowers and black leaves.

The leaves were painted in freehand and using a different level of ink that shows the vividness of life. The small leaves beside the big ones are diverse in number. The red flowers and the yellow pistils are very striking and heavy, nearly bending the lotus's petiole. So, the picture suggests movement. It was painted in 1948 when Qi was 84 years of age.

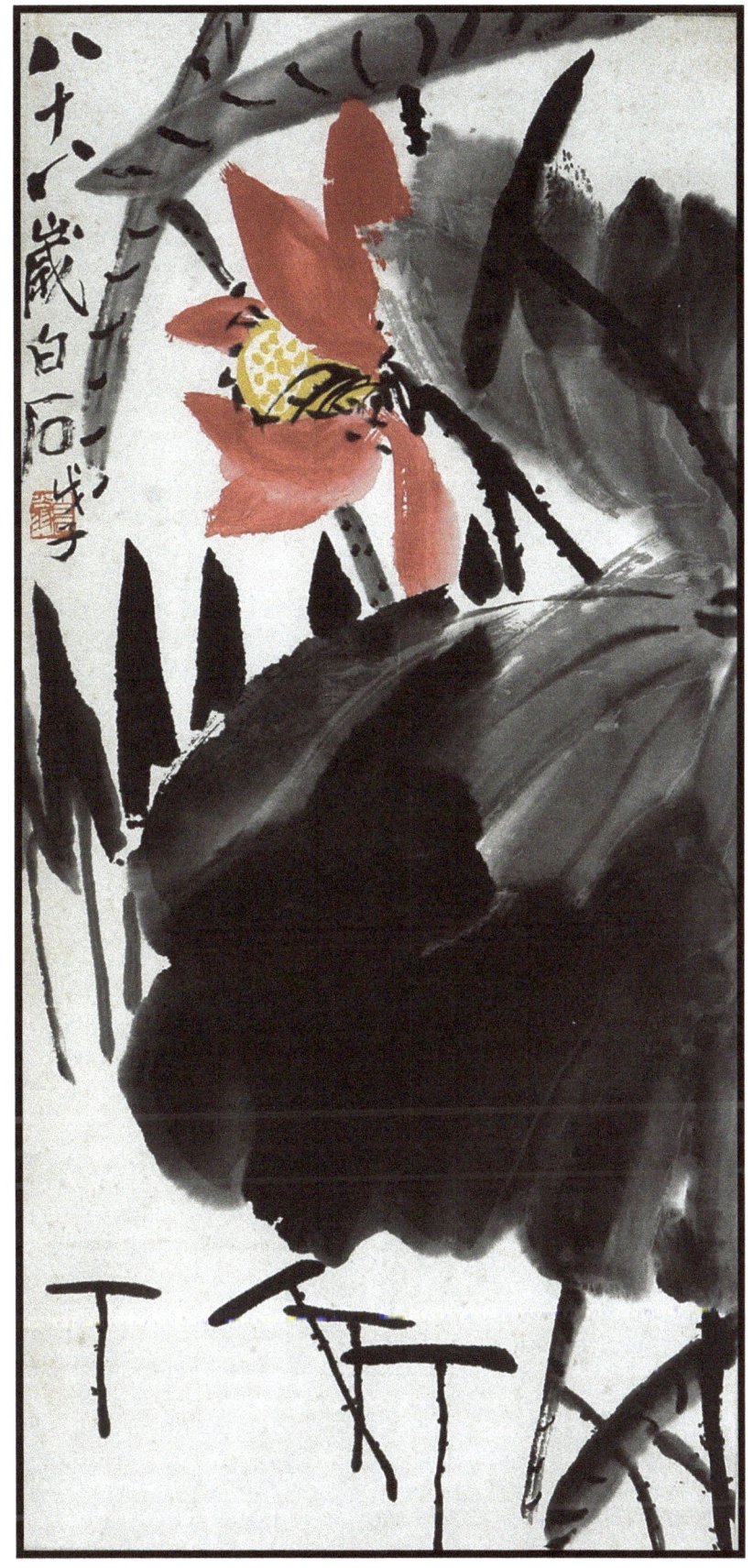

Image 2-14: Lotus

Chapter Three: The Works of Qi Baishi 2

1. Chicks and Morning Glories

Inscription: Jiping elder Qi Baishi painted in Beijing.

Read Seal: 85 years of age.

Description:

The morning glory is a common subject for Qi. The reason why he loved to paint it is possibly because they seem to grow so tall, almost 'up to the sky'. This Qi thought was a symbol of a positive spirit and attitude.

The picture is different to others of the same plant. First is the contrast in colour. Qi usually painted the morning glory in a red colour, but this time he used an indigo instead. The intention of doing this was perhaps to offset it against the three striking yellow chicks. The vigorous bamboo pole, the twisted vine and the flexible petiole all emboy Qi's superb painting skills, which gives them a vivid, life-like quality. From the red seal, we know that this picture was painted in 1945.

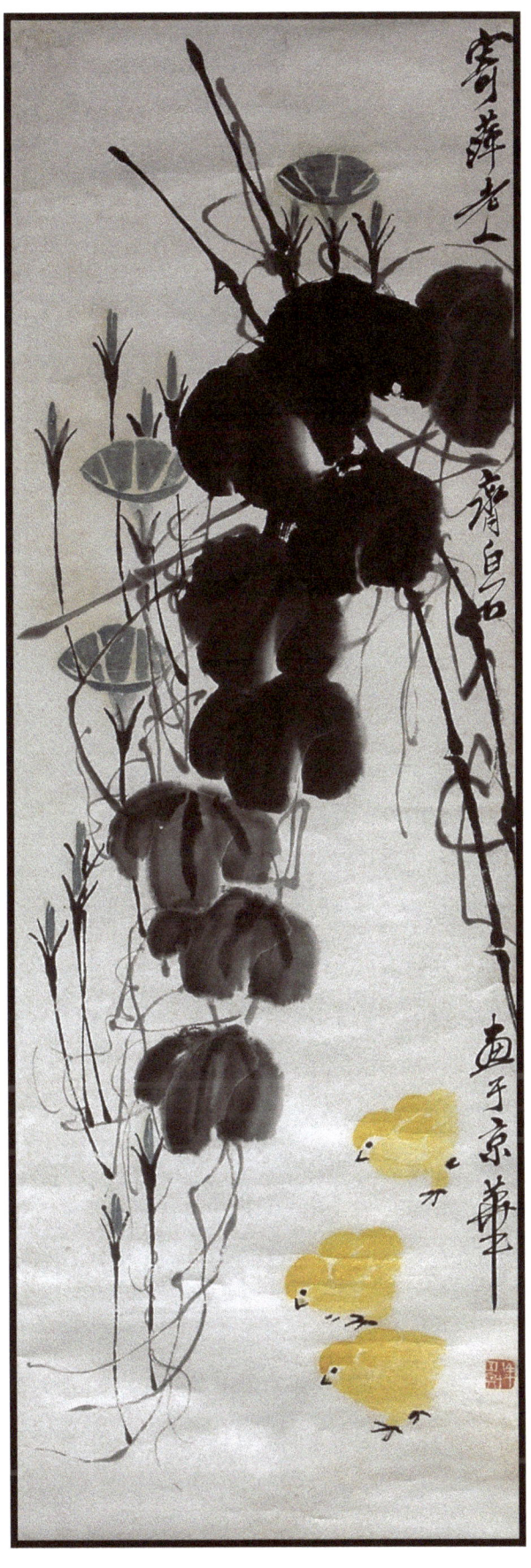

Image 3-1: Chicks and Morning Glories

2. Chrysanthemum and Longevity

Inscription: Elder Baishi painted in Beijing at 88 years of age.

Read Seal: Qi Baishi. Dreaming of a pond of fish swimming in my hometown.

Description:

Peach, chrysanthemum, jars and locusts are all common subjects for Qi. As soon as you see the imagery, you might think of the style of Wu Changshuo, who was a very famous artist in contemporary China. These were also favourite subjects for his paintings. If we compare Qi and Wu's works, we can find similarities in the ways of painting peach and chrysanthemum and the use of colour.

What is the difference between them? The spirit. Wu is a literary man but Qi is a farmer. Qi's painting style didn't use a regular method but was more open and unaffected. You can see this in his sketching of a basket and jar, which are very straightforward and uncomplicated.

So, while Qi was happy to adopt styles from others, he still retained and created his own unique style and character. In China, if you can give up the pursuit of pleasure you will attain longevity equal to the extent that the chrysanthemum is fragrant. The peach also represents longevity. A locust is jumping on to the basket, creating some movement.

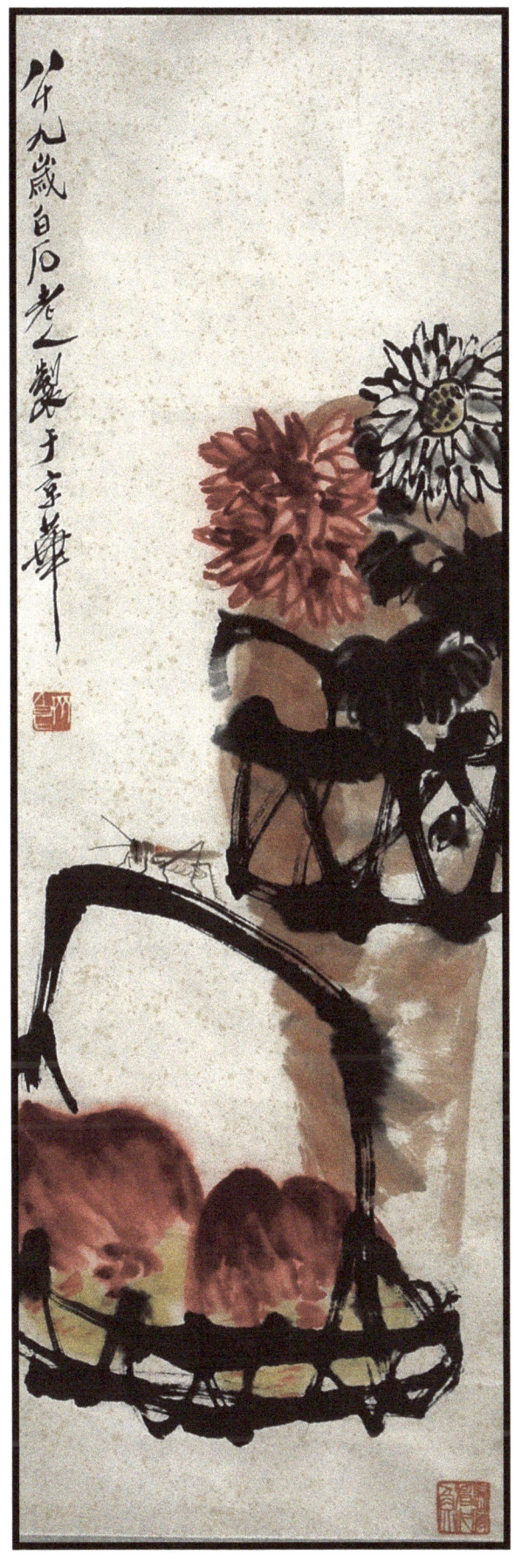

Image 3-2: Chrysanthemum and Longevity

3.   **Longevity 1**

Inscription: Prolong Life.

Qi Baishi painted it at 88 years of age and carved the four words.

Read Seal: Qi Baishi. I am 88 years of age. I am doing what I like to do

Qi Baishi: "I am 88 years of age. I am happy because I can still paint."

Description:

Life is an eternal topic for human study. Qi drew a basket of chrysanthemums, two paradise flycatcher birds and a bee to embody and put life into this picture. The Chinese for the paradise flycatcher is pronounced 'shou dai niao' and 'shou' is a homophone of longevity, which introduces the theme. Qi used a very 'comfortable' and lively way to depict such a serious theme.

One paradise flycatcher is jumping on to the basket while the other is standing on the ground, but both are staring at a point outside of the picture. What are they looking for? Maybe it is another beautiful bird. In China, it was believed that if you could refrain from the sole pursuit of pleasure then your longevity would be commensurate to the extent that the chrysanthemum is fragrant.

A person only gets to the truth, however, once they grow old. This picture was painted when Qi was 88 years of age. Through this colourful and diverse piece of art, we can feel that he was still full of energy and life at this age.

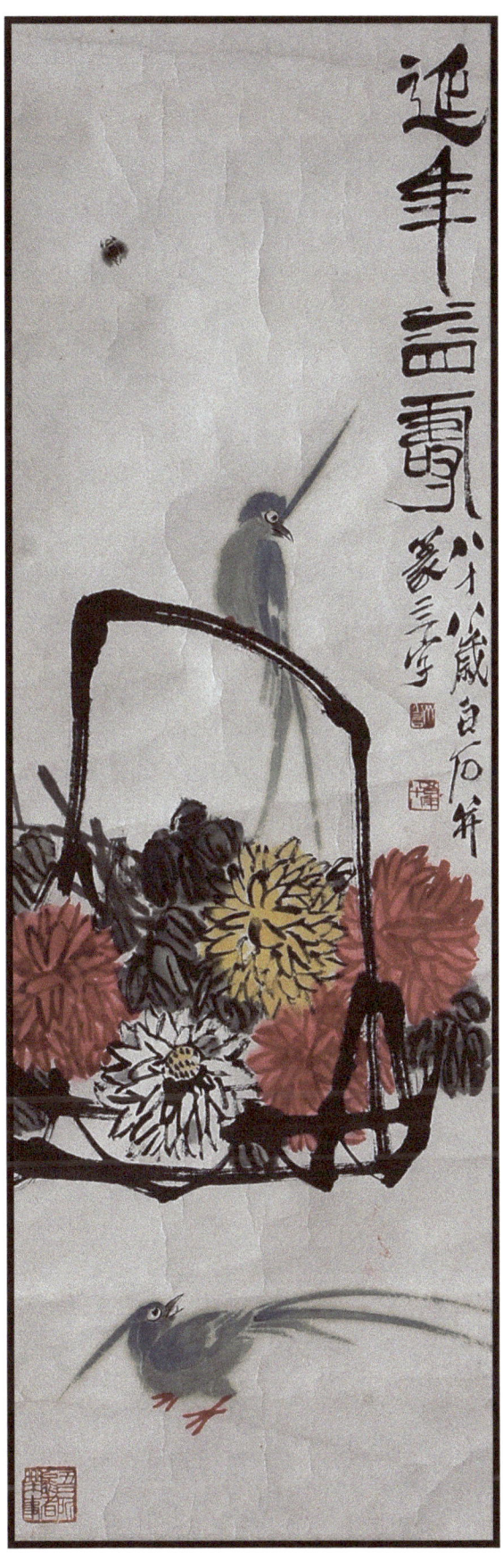

Image 3-3: Longevity 1

4. Wisteria

Inscription: My home-town friends Kejian, please give me some advice. Baishi was 93 years of age.

Read Seal: Baishi.

Description:
Each distinguished artist has his or her own secret. Different backgrounds provide different secrets. Qi had been a farmer, so his works were resonant with village scenes. Sometimes, even if he did not draw village subjects, we can still feel his natural, unsophisticated village character in his works. They are lively and interesting, which originates from his life and his child-like nature. Ordinary people can understand his paintings and feel that they are 'friendly', relate to their lives and remind them of something in their youth.

The leaves are diverse and disorderly and the wisterias are gently dangling down. The vines are unruly and unaffected. All of them receive sunshine and dew from the beauty of nature. So, we can imagine a cloudless world with a gentle wind which is free and unrestrained. Qi's art can combine the sophisticated and unsophisticated, producing a rural, elegant, literary folk-like effect.

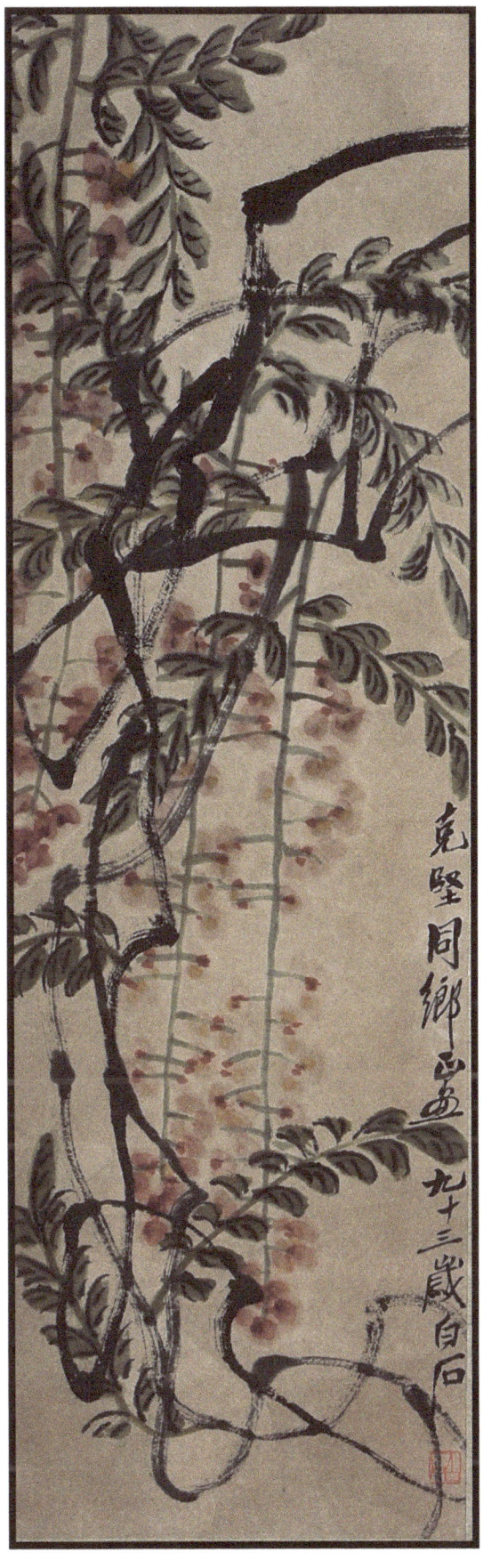

Image 3-4: Wisteria

5. 800 Years of Longevity

Inscription: 800 years' longevity.

Read Seal: Qi Da.

Description:

Myna and cypress are pronounced 'ba ge' and 'bai shu' respectively in Chinese, which is a homophone of 'ba bai', and means 800 years. This is a picture of a blessing of longevity and a portrayal of life. It shows the cursive script style in Qi's rough sketches. Look at the dots for the foliage. They are unruly and unrestrained and embody Qi's calligraphy skills.

In this painting, Qi broke the rules. He painted the branches first and then those disorderly dots. The myna, which is looking at the trees, is just like a human being and is thinking about something. There is a subversive element that resides in Qi's nature.

When he was young and was learning to paint, Qi imitated the traditional arts and followed their rules. When he got to middle age, his paintings became humorous and ironic. When he was old, he didn't obey the rules anymore and created his own style. This was not just a challenge to traditional painting. I think that maybe breaking the rules excited Qi, making him happy, and showed his pursuit of freedom and his uninhibited character.

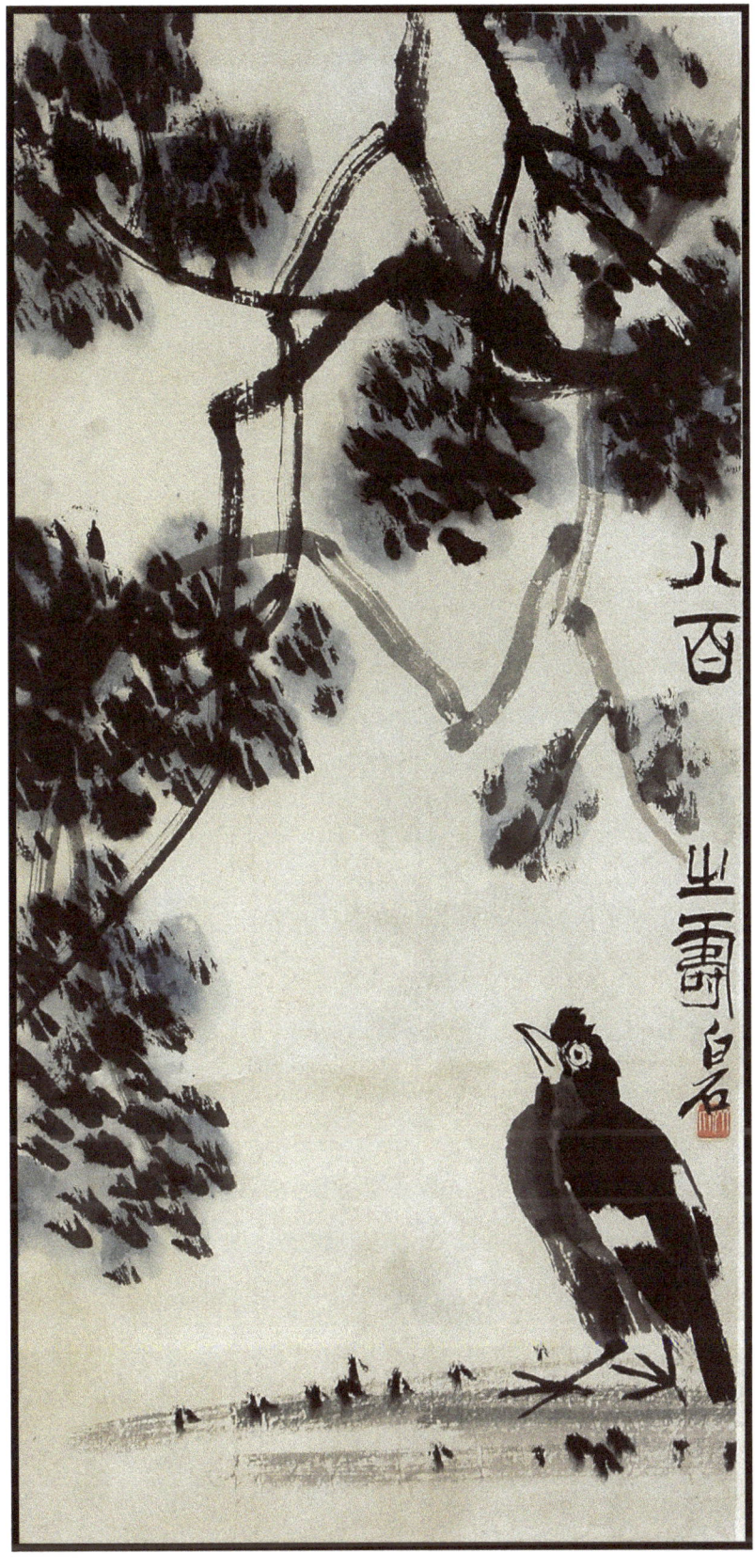

Image 3-5: 800 Years of Longevity

6. Loofah

Inscription:
Comrade Huaiming, please give me some advice. In Renchen year, Baishi was 92 years of age.

Read Seal: Qi Baishi.

Description:
Every time you look at Qi's works, you feel happy. This is because his painting style is flexible and balanced in perspective and theme. Sometimes, we even seem to smell the fragrance of the lotus, hear the buzzing of the bees and the whispering of the mandarin ducks.

Qi's emotion was always connected closely with the village, farming and country life. Some subjects that were previously thought to be vulgar by former artists became acceptable and popular after being drawn by Qi. He even created a new field of Chinese art.

In this picture, the leaves are big and juicy, the bamboo poles have many joints, the vines are twisted, and the loofahs are of different shapes. The most striking objects are the yellow flowers; these are very shiny and attractive. So, Qi succeeded in producing a rural display in front of us. Perhaps this just represented recollections from his early life. When he painted this picture in Beijing he was 92 years of age. He had always deeply missed, for his whole life, his cloudless home-town skyline with its gentle breeze.

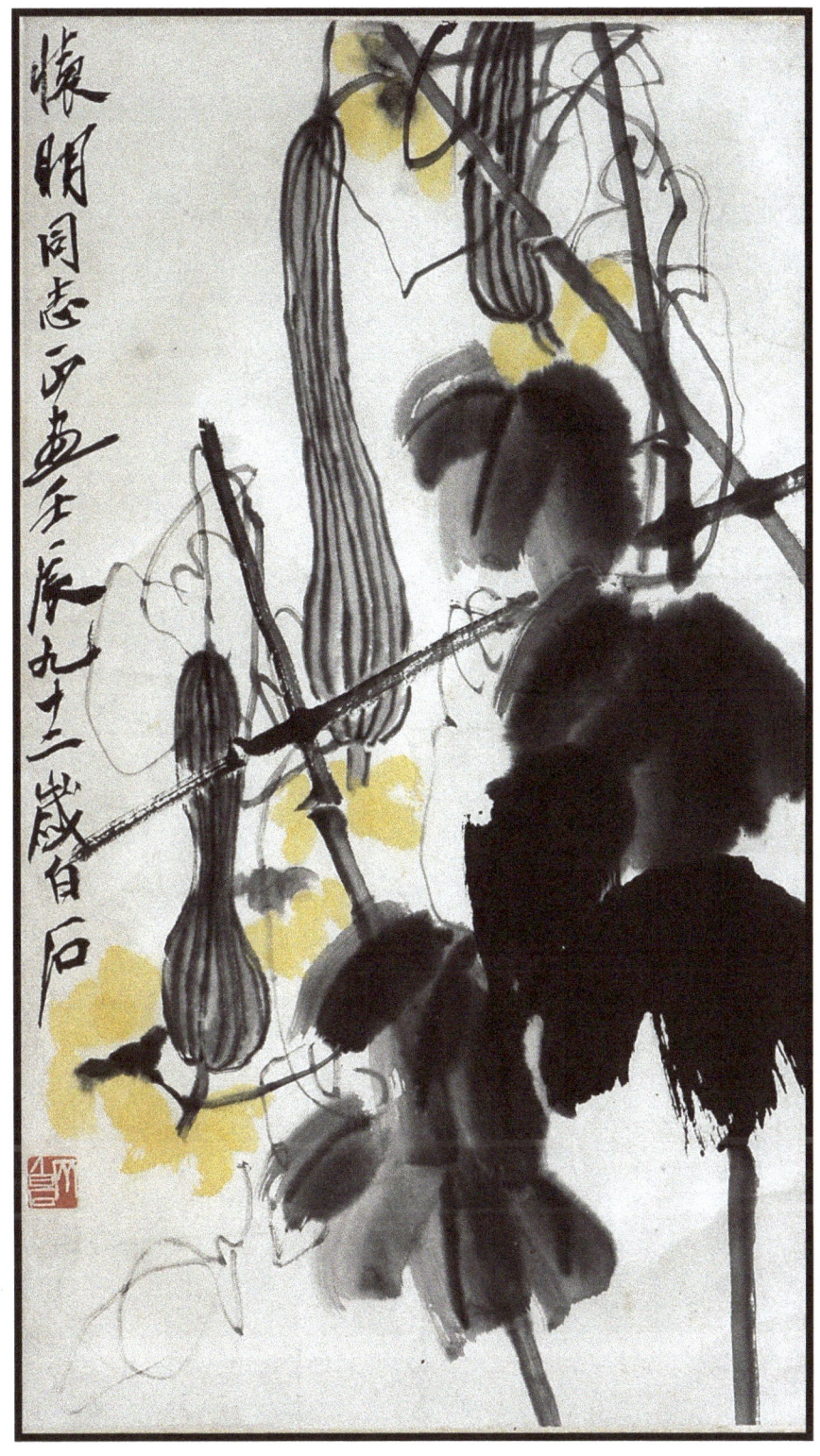

Image 3-6: Loofah

7. Morning Glories and Dragonfly

Inscription: Mr Haixing, please receive it. In Kuiwei year, the older Baishi painted in Beijing at 83 years of age.

Read Seal: Elder farmer of Hunan.

Description:

Mei Lanfang was a very popular opera star in China, who was Qi's friend and student. Once, when Qi went to Mei Lanfang's house, he saw a morning glory blooming as big as a bowl. From that moment on, he began to paint them bigger.

The leaves are painted in a very simple but diverse way. Qi painted the flowers very carefully. They are more complicated than the leaves, not only relating to the shape but also to the spacing of the petioles.

The vines are drawn using a cursive script style with superb skill and attention to detail, so, although they are numerous, they are both orderly and vibrant. The dragonfly is in flight and is very lively.

Qi designed the whole image just with the right level of detail. The flowerpot, flowers, vines, leaves, bamboo poles, dragonfly, calligraphy and seals; all the elements are arranged very well. If he had added just one dot, it would have been too complicated, if he had moved one element, it would have been disorderly. This is a very good example of the Daoist philosophy of wu wei: natural action.

Everybody praises Qi's skill in using pen and ink, but we think that this arrangement is his best.

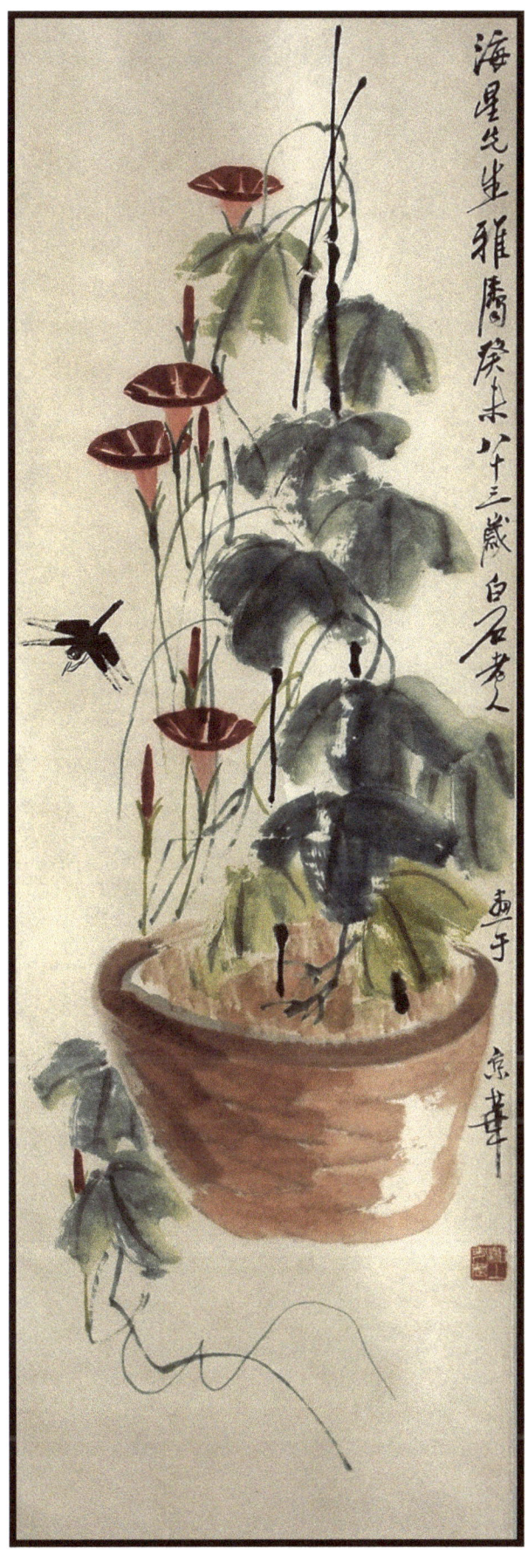

Image 3-7: Morning Glories and Dragonfly

8. Magnolia Flower

Preface Calligraphy:
Mr Yaobing, please receive it. Elder Baishi painted in March of Kuiwei year.

Read Seal: Qi Da.

Description:
Qi Baishi loved magnolia flowers for two reasons. The first is that they are fragrant – even indoors. The second is that they are the first blossoms of spring. The magnolia flowers are sketched with lines that are smooth and sophisticated. Their delineation is orderly and clear. When Qi started to paint, he thought about the arrangement carefully. As he painted, he utilised a fluent and leisurely style.

Qi mostly used the middle of the Chinese brush but also used the side and often both. Even when he was painting during a social engagement, he would put his emotions into his work. Qi put it succinctly: "Painting should be uplifting to those looking at it. If someone cannot use the middle of the Chinese brush freely, it is because he or she is lacking in talent."

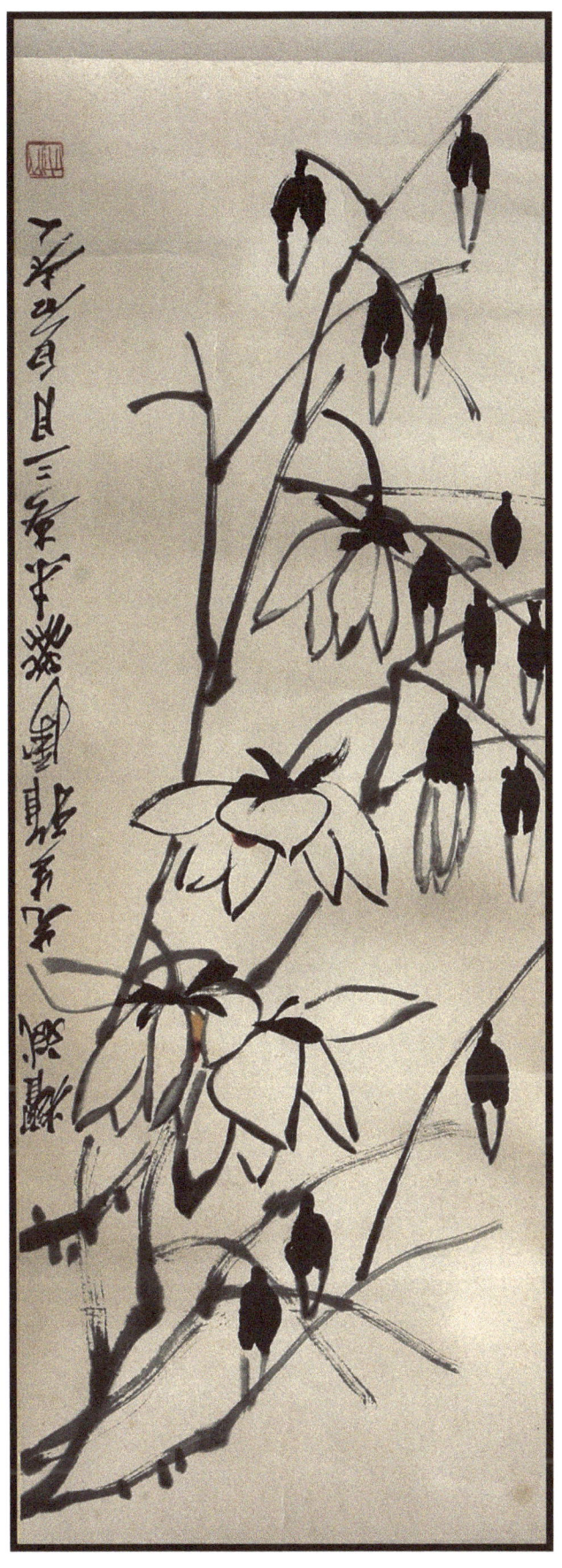

Image 3-8: Magnolia Flower

9. Lotus

Preface Calligraphy: Jieshan Elder painted it at 86 years of age.

Read Seal: Baishi. Xiangtan people. Wang and Fan were gone and this just left Qi Da alone.

Description:

The picture was painted using smooth but carefree strokes, without any hesitation. The colours used are heavy and the gradation is clear. This creates a natural expression and is typical of Qi's painting of red flowers and black leaves.

The most marvellous thing is the arrangement of the picture. First is the positioning of the large and small leaves, the petioles and the flowers. The density, gradation, direction and shape are perfectly synchronised using both imagination and reality, and flexibility.

Second is the relationship between the colour and the ink. It would be boring if only the flower were red, so Qi carved two read seals stamped under the flower to correspond with them. The gradation is obvious now and the artistic conception is profound. Qi loved the lotus flower; he painted each side of it to make it look as though the flower is smiling.

Qi even invited his friends to celebrate a birthday party for the lotus blossoming.

Somebody once said that painting reflects one's heart. When Qi was alive, he held a lot of exhibitions in Nanjing and Shanghai, which were greatly enjoyed by many people and increased his popularity. He painted this picture when he was 86 years of age.

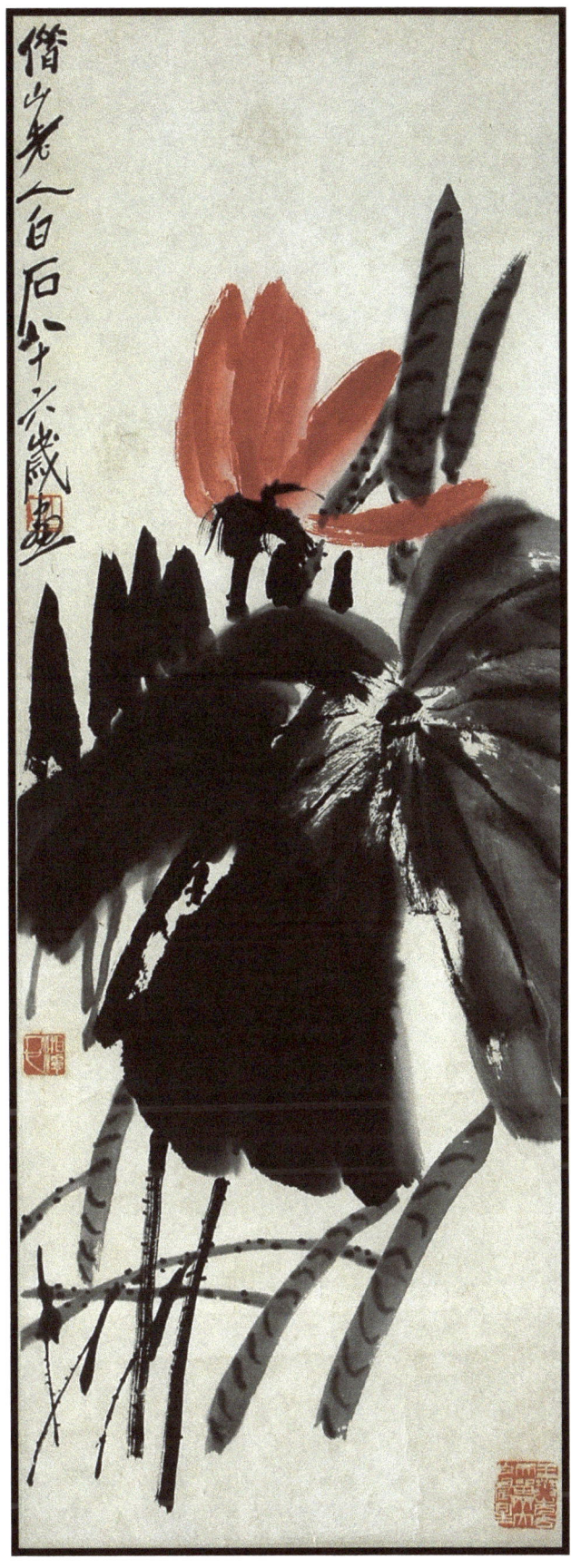

Image 3-9: Lotus

10. **Longevity 2**

Preface Calligraphy: Longevity. Baishi was 90 years of age in Gengyin year.

Read Seal: Baishi.

Description:

What is the point of Chinese art? It is its romantic charm. Qi used free-hand brush work, giving life and energy to the subjects he painted. His paintings focused on the 'spirit', with not too much concern about the shape. Somebody said that Qi's paintings 'sit in the middle' between similarities and dissimilarities. This picture simply depicts a brunch of chrysanthemums.

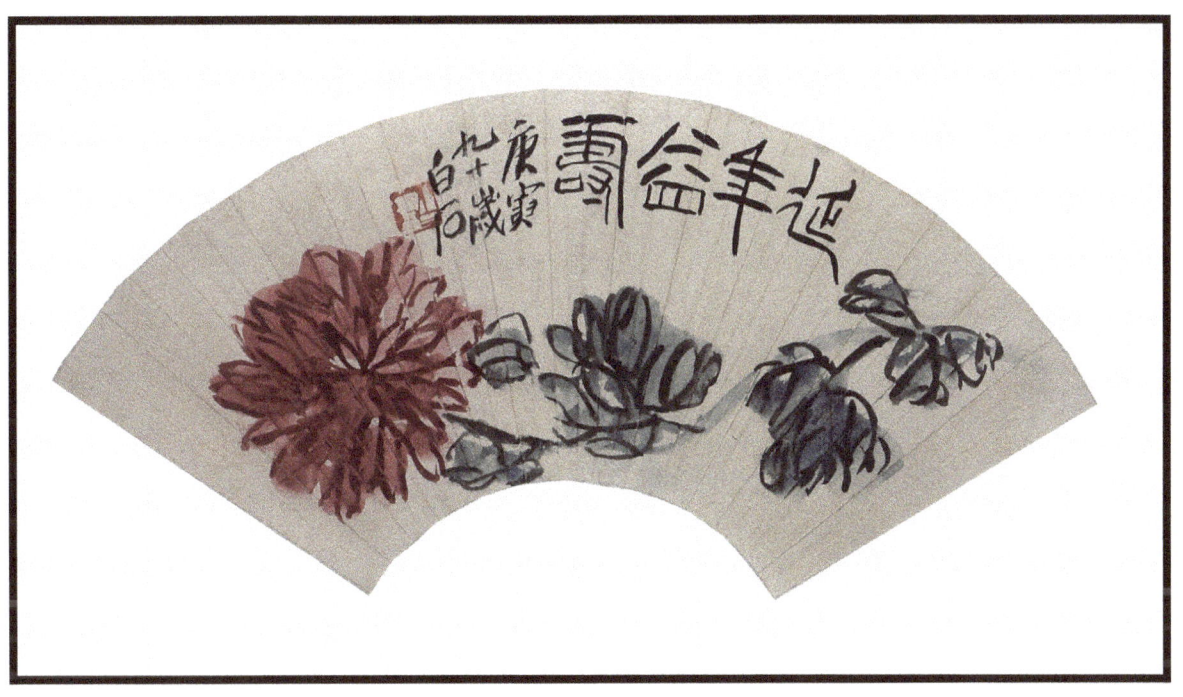

Image 3-10: Longevity 2

11. Lucid Ganoderma

Preface Calligraphy: Longevity. Please receive it Mr Suichu. Elder Baishi painted in Beijing in the Gengchen year.

Read Seal: Qi Da.

Description:

The ganoderma lucidum, or 'lingzhi' mushroom in Chinese, has been used for medicinal purposes in traditional Chinese medicine for more than two thousand years.

This is a good example of Qi's strong artistic ability. The paper fan is hard to paint because there are a lot of pleats in it. He has used its features cleverly to allow the fragrant thoroughwort to lighten the imagery, emphasising vigour and vitality.

Look at the longest leaves, and you will see that they are painted from right to left according to their own natural direction. Qi painted the front and the back of the leaves naturalistically, using both heavy and light penstrokes where required.

There are three bright ganodermas in the picture, that were painted with the same consistency used for the leaves, and each possessing its own character. On the left of the picture there is the prefaced calligraphy upon which was written the word 'longevity'. The left side echoes the right side, the density echoes emptiness.

It looks as though Qi has painted this with little difficulty but he has had to call on his vast experience and superb skills.

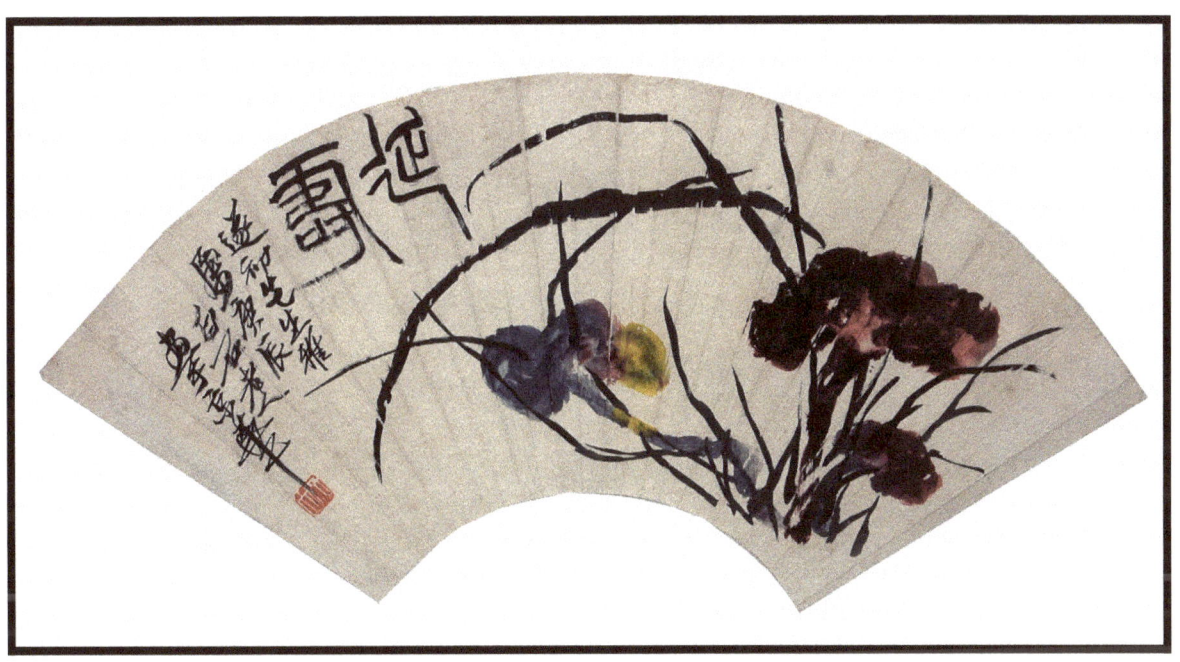

Image 3-11: Lucid Ganoderma

12. Peony and Vase

Preface Calligraphy: Best wishes to Mr Kuizhong. 84 years of age Qi Huang. Moving fortune to safety. Vase has its shape but the safety is hidden. I wrote this again and used the pronunciation of vase, meaning peaceful life.

Read Seal: Baishi, Qida.

Description:

The peony symbolises fortune in China. The pronunciation of the word 'vase' in Chinese is homophonic with the word for safety. This picture was painted in 1944 when Japan invaded China and Qi's home town of Xiangtan was occupied on 17 June of that year. Qi painted a group of mice satirising the Japanese aggressors and cursing them with bad luck. Qi painted this picture to send a cherished message of peace to his friend during the harsh wartime period.

The vase was painted using freehand brush work, and the peonies were painted bursting into full bloom. The pistil was painted in more detail.

A painting like this needs some detail in freehand and some small brushwork that should be used freely. Qi painted peonies even when he was 96 years old, and this shows that his success was due not only to his talent but also to his hard work.

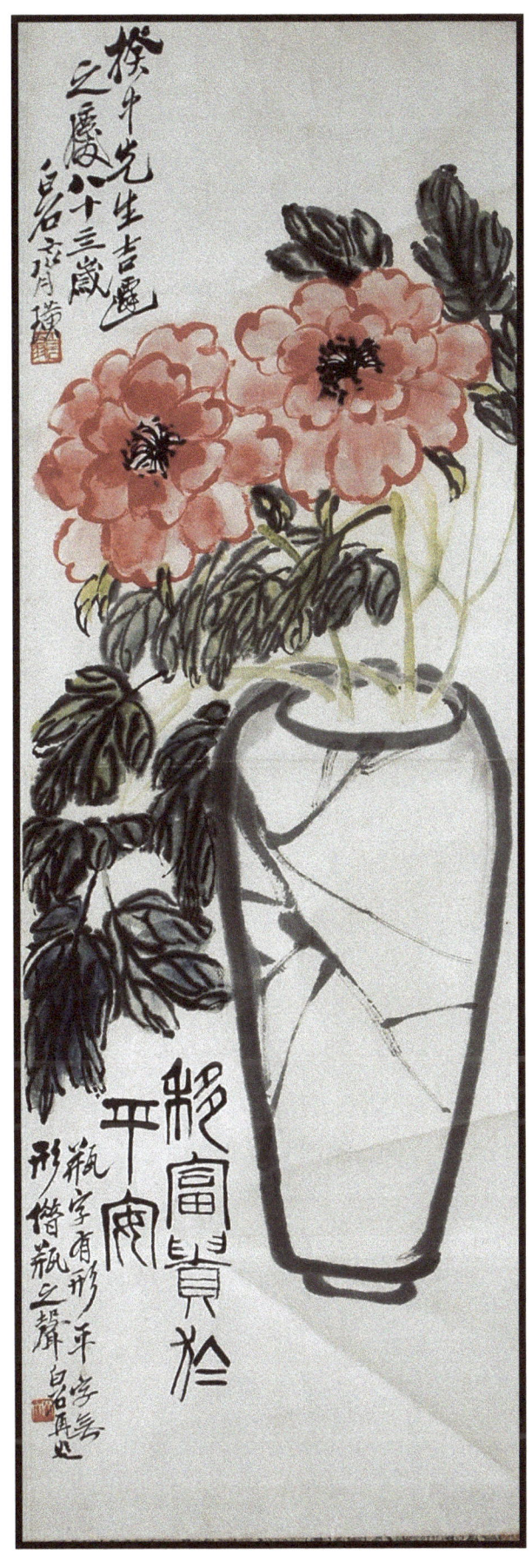

Image 3-12: Peony and Vase

13. Chrysanthemum and Autumn Insect

Preface Calligraphy: My niece please enjoy it. 89 years of age Baishi.

Read Seals: Baishi. Longevity.

Description:

Plum blossom, orchid, bamboo and chrysanthemum are often described by the Chinese as the 'four gentlemen among flowers'. Chrysanthemum blossoms in autumn alone and its character is light and 'self-reliant, elegant in looks but light in taste and never bowing to any power'.

Qi painted this picture when he was 85 years of age. This was in 1949 and the year that new Republic of China was established. Qi felt very happy and started a new period for his art. He painted two red chrysanthemums and one white one in this picture. It is obvious that the two red ones are the focus and that each has its own character. Qi painted the leaves with vibrancy. The chrysanthemum is 'quiet' but the insect is dynamic. The leaves look as though they are moving with the wind. So, stillness echoes movement, the leaves are quiet in movement and movement reflects stillness. This is the secret of Qi Baishi.

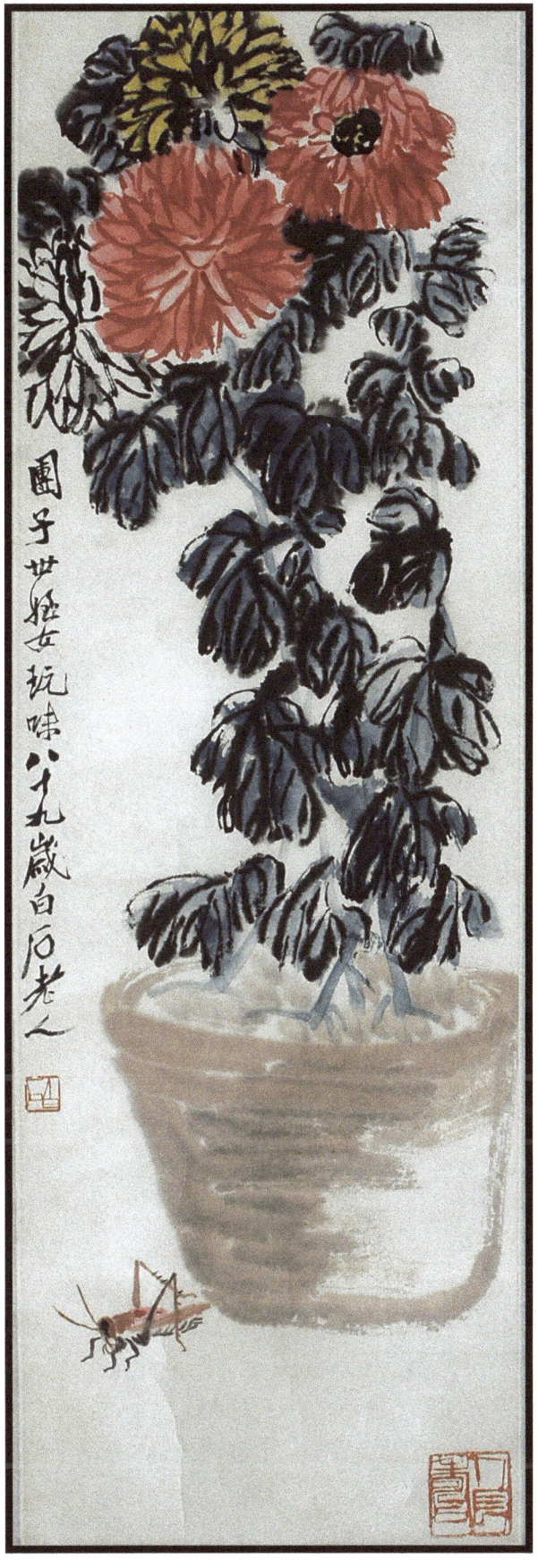

Image 3-13: Chrysanthemum and Autumn Insect

Chapter Four: The Works of Qi Baishi 3

1. Qi Baozhu

Seal Margin: My wife Baozhu asked for a seal. Elder Baishi Shanweng.

Description:

Baozhu was Qi's second wife, who was born into a poor family in Sichuan province in 1902. After Qi's first wife, Chen Chunjun, died, Qi elevated Baozhu to be the first in status. They lived together for more than twenty years and loved each other deeply. The seal had Qi Baozhu's name carved on it, which is drawn flat and wide like a picture. The Chinese words on it are deeply embedded. Qi used emphasis appropriate to the meaning of each word with sharp, strong carving marks.

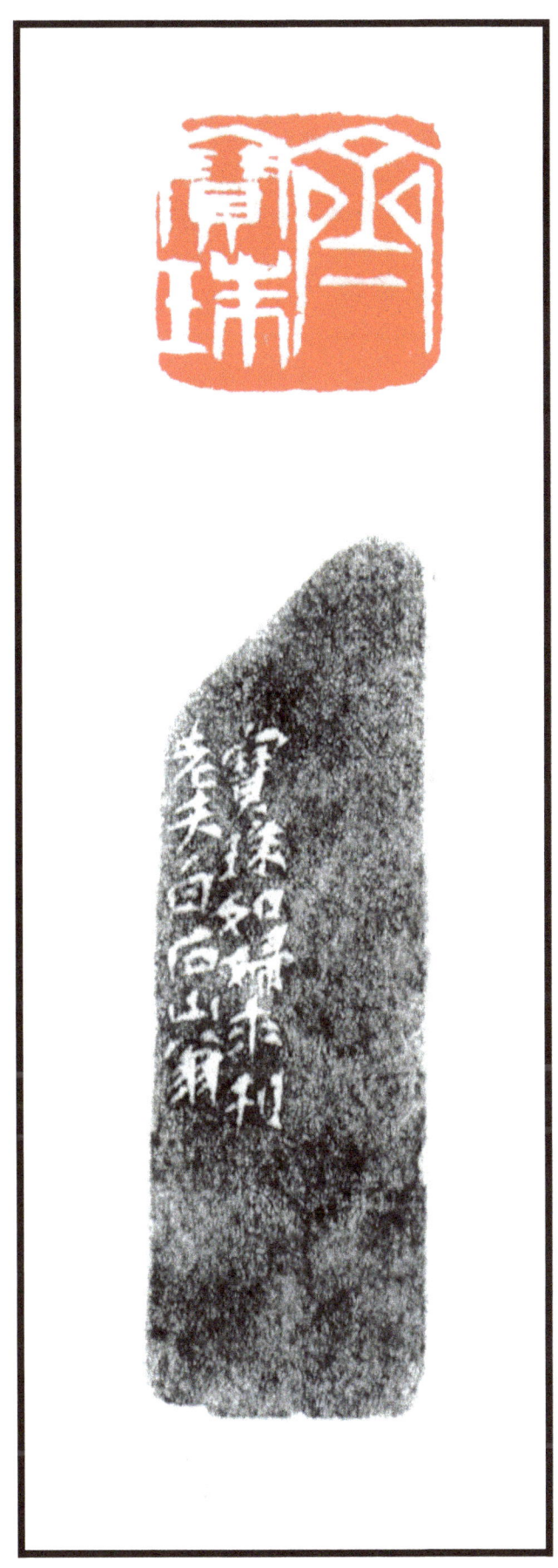

Image 4-1: Qi Baozhu

2. Light

Seal Margin: This is the nickname of my wife Baozhu after she was 40 years of age. Baishi.

Description:

This seal was made around 1942 and was carved from right to left. The design looks as though it veers to the right and the upper part is more emphasised than the lower part. So, vitality echoes reality, which is forceful and graceful. The face of the seal is substantial, full of design and content.

Qi applied more energy on the last stroke of 'guang' (the right character), which is an ancient Chinese method of carving. This ancient method, combined with his creativity, has some harmonious changes but does not look as though it is too sharp. This is perhaps his most iconic seal.

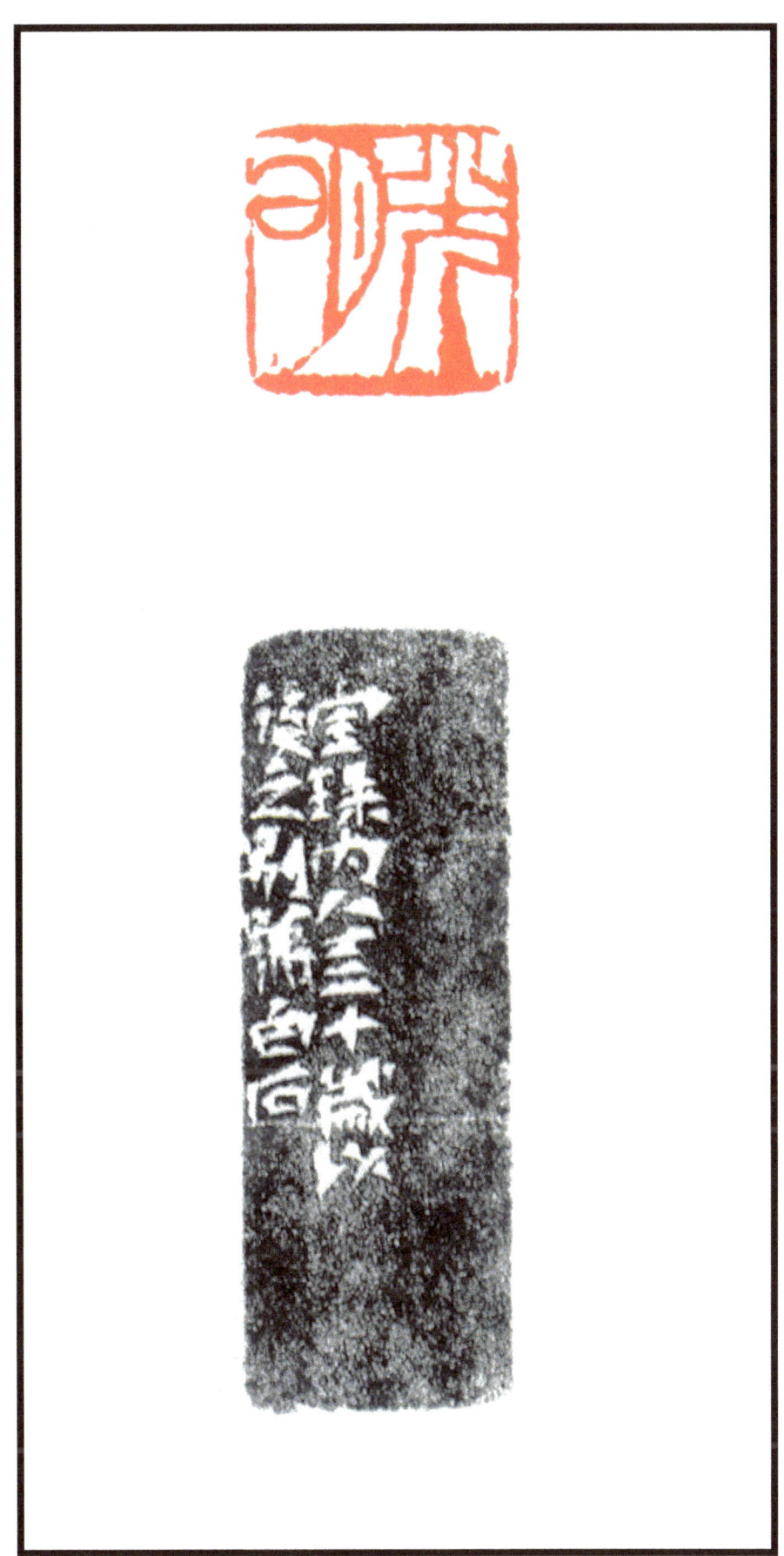

Image 4-2: Light

3. Dingchao

Seal Margin: Baishi

Description:

There are two kinds of seal in China: zhuwen and baiwen. Zhuwen is translated as 'red character seal'. The stone is carved so that the Chinese character is raised, and, when red ink is applied, the character appears red against a white background. Baiwen is translated as 'white character seal'. Here, the character is carved into the stone, so the application of red ink leaves the character as white against a red background.

This is a red character seal that was carved by Qi with an inventive mind. The two characters represent a person's name, which alternate with each other and use the space efficiently. The opposite angles echo one another and enhance their relevance. His design is perfect but he makes it look as though it is unintentional. This comes from his great insight, enabling him to create such a wonderful and natural piece of work.

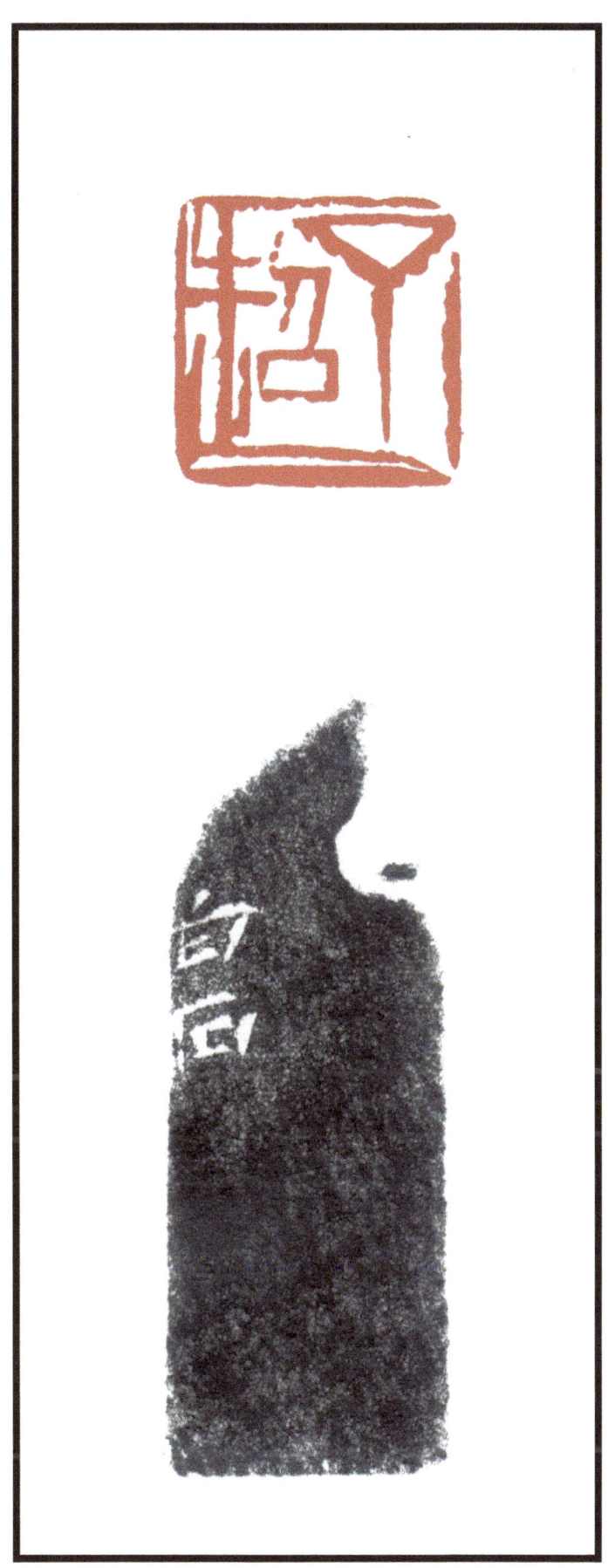

Image 4-3: Dingchao

4. Modesty

Seal Margin: Baishi.

Description:

This is a white character seal with only one character on it and with no variation. If there is no variation, it is hard for it to look energetic. The left side of the seal is more complicated than the right, so the left is virtual while the right is real. But Qi alternates and the orderly structure enables us to feel that the internal space is narrow and that the outside is wide.

China is known as 'the nation of ancient customs', and being friendly and modest with someone are two traditional virtues among the Chinese. Qi always retained his modesty throughout his whole life even though he accomplished so much within the art field. He always remembered that he was an ordinary peasant who had been born in Xiangtan county. Throughout his life, he deeply loved his home town.

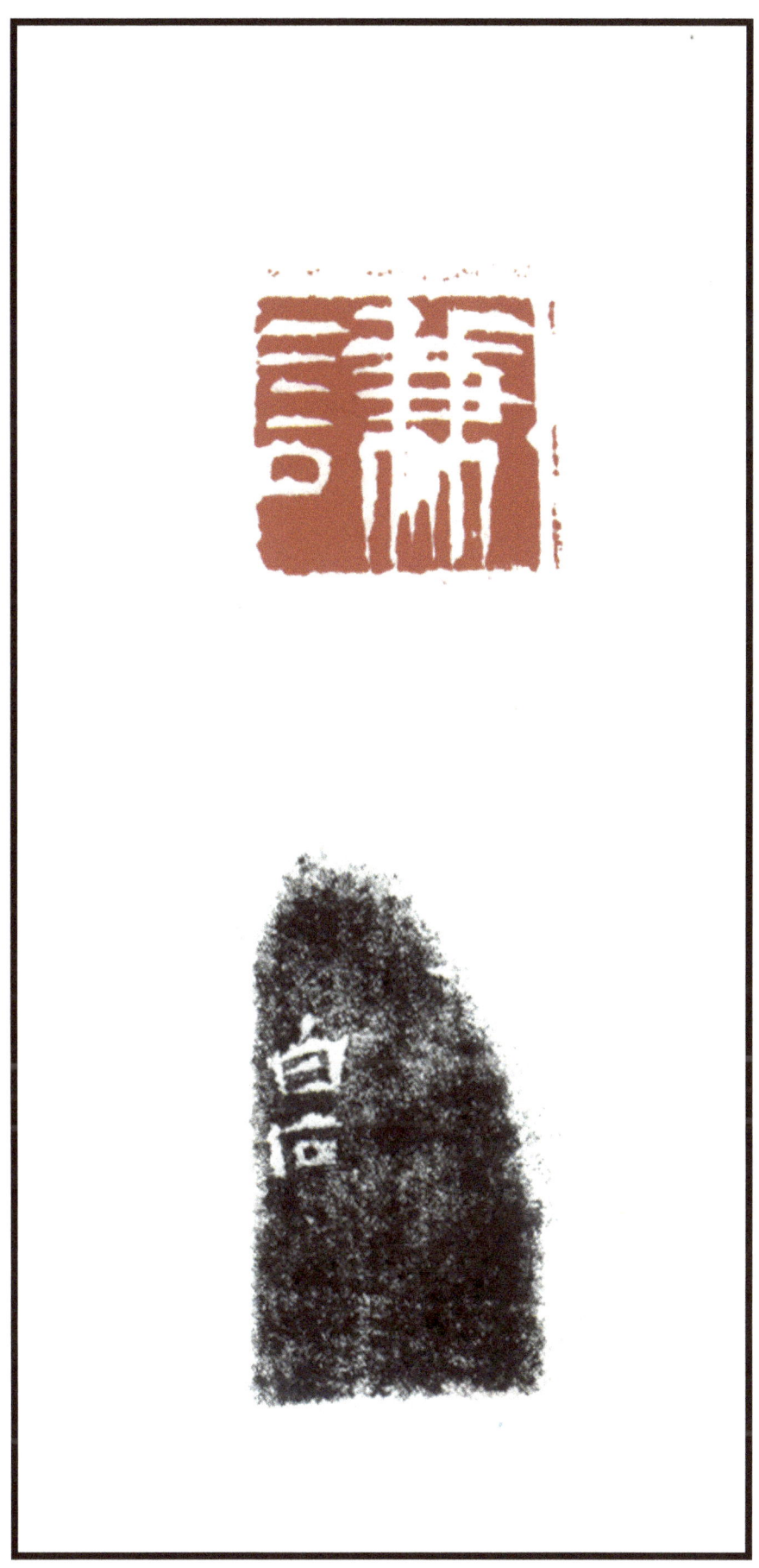

Image 4-4: Modesty

5. Tool box

Description:

This is a tool box made of wood. The box was made by Qi around the period between 1882 and 1902 when he was working as a carpenter, and it measures 35.4mm x 22mm x 28.5mm. When Qi was 15 years of age, he started to learn rough carpentry and how to carve designs. Nowadays, there are few woodcarvings left in the world that were made by Qi. Most of what we see on the market is shoddy substitutes.

This tool box was originally kept in Qi's house and then transferred to his granddaughter's during the war. On the lifting yoke on the top of the box was carved a dragon, and there are four drawers in the front. The three colours in the box are black, red and yellow. Qi carved a cloud, a dragon and some ancient figures on the two side faces. These are all auspicious patterns in China. One side is 'Number One Scholar' and the other side is 'Unicorn Appearance'.

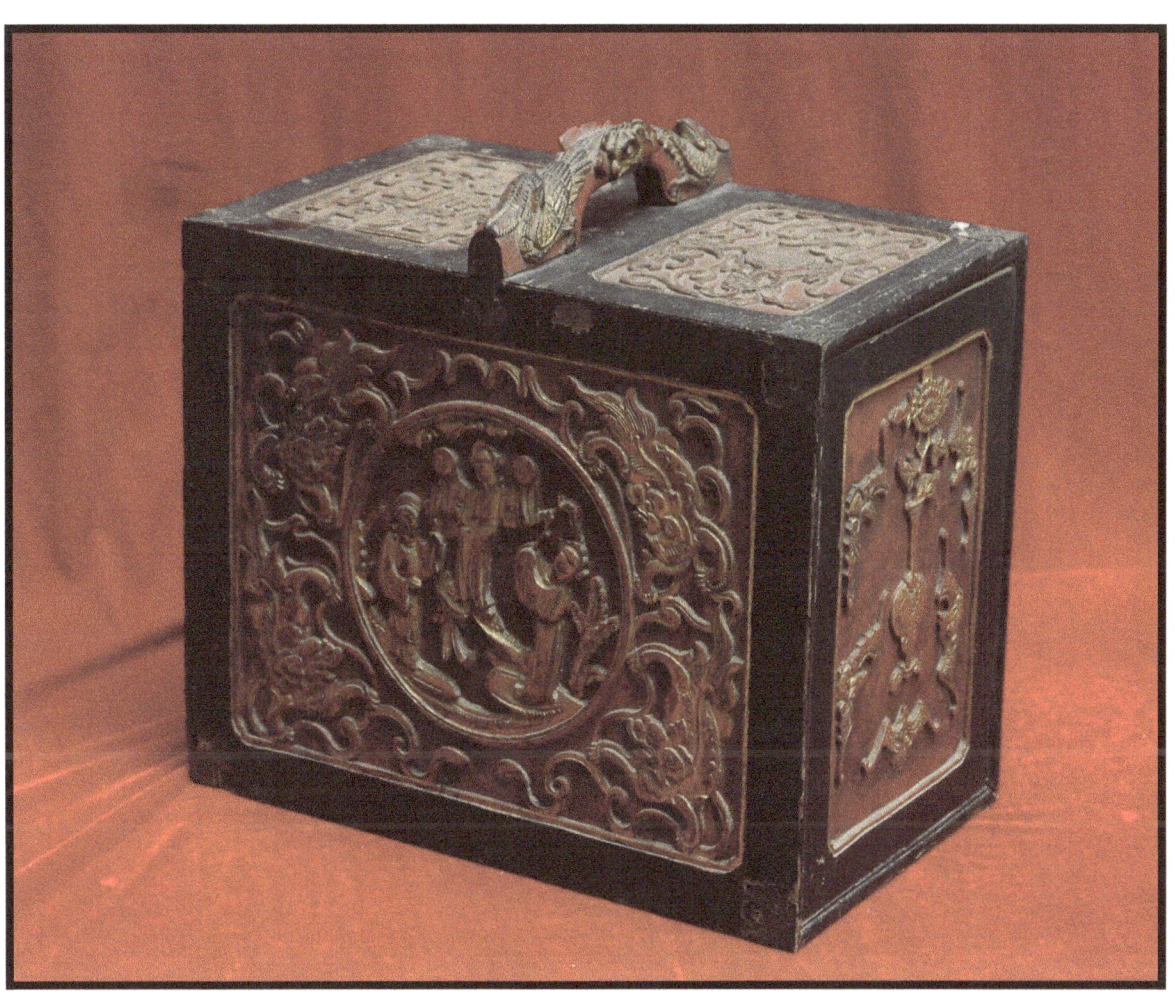

Image 4-5: Tool Box

6. The Bed Frame

This is a carved bed frame. In those days, beds in Hunan were often made of camphorwood and were painted red, yellow and black. Usually, the figures on the bed frames at that time were short and had big heads and wide faces. The faces are raised in the carving and differ from each other. The dress for each person is simple but graceful. There are three groups of patterns in this frame. In the middle of the frame, there are patterns on the roof, and lanterns and columns in what looks like a drawing room.

There are eleven people in the room. In the middle are two elders, who are wearing a royal crown and a phoenix coronet. There are some men and women talking and standing around them. In front of the desk there are two young people, and the girl looks as though she is bowing to the elder.

This depicts a very famous story in China called 'Congratulations to Guo Ziyi on his birthday'. Guo Ziyi was a revered general in the Tang dynasty, who won many wars and was deeply respected by later generations. There are some other patterns in the other two sides of the frame on which are carved pine trees, stones, hills, ponds and figures.

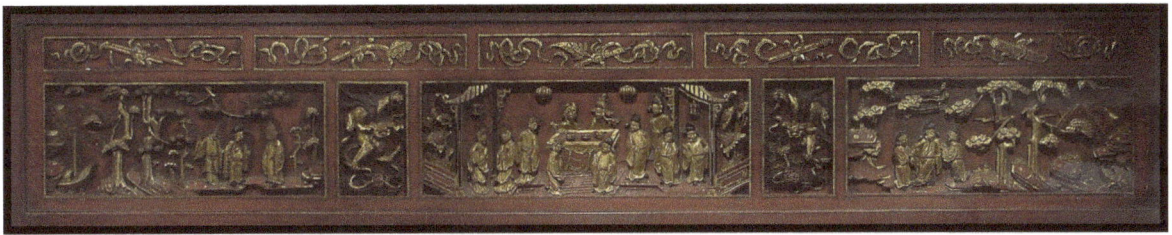

Image 4-6: The Bed Frame

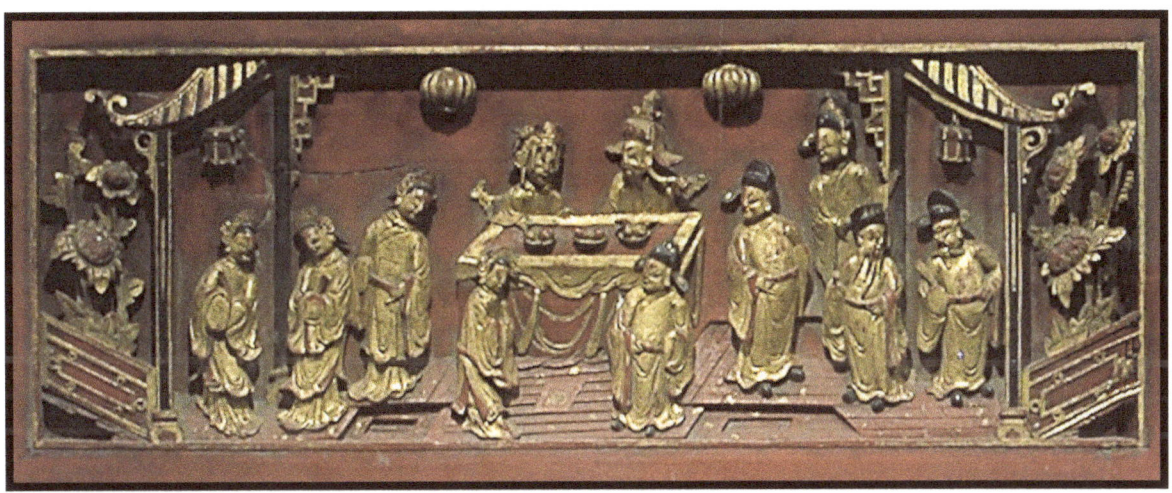

Image 4-6a: The Bed Frame Centre Panel

7. Carved Stone and Bamboo

Description:

This photograph shows some of Qi's carvings: two carved stone screens and three carved bamboo brush pots. The two carved stone screens are of similar size; these are puce and carved with cameos. One carving shows a plum tree with lots of winter blossom. The other is also a carving of a plum tree and winter blossom that is in full bloom. There is also some bamboo. A magpie sits on the plum tree. This has an auspicious meaning because the magpie is a lucky bird in China. On the back of the carved stone screen there is an inscription that states that this was a gift sent to Qi's teacher, Wang Kanyun, when Qi was 40 years of age.

The three bamboo brush pots are carved with leaves with calligraphy on them. Since ancient times, the plum blossom, orchid, bamboo and chrysanthemum have become spiritual symbols for the Chinese, who use them to reflect their moods, feelings and hopes. The qualities of the plum blossom are those of being proud and self-reliant. The quality of bamboo is firm and yet not seeking fortune and gain. Qi occasionally carved, even after he had become a painter.

Qi's carpentry complemented his painting because he grasped the shape and quality of flowers, birds, insects, fish and other objects when he was training to become a carpenter. His carving skill also helped his painting and seal cutting.

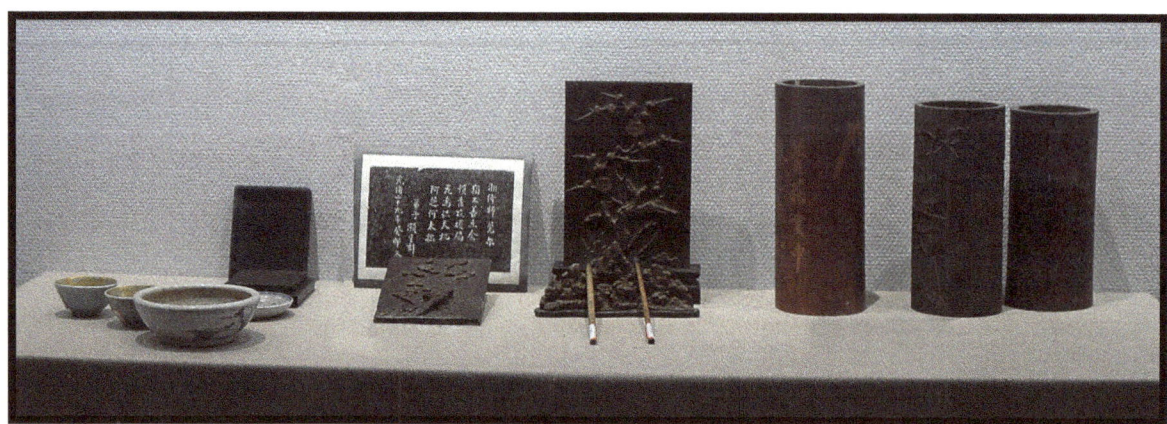

Image 4-7: Carved Stone and Bamboo

Chapter Five: Pablo Picasso

Pablo Picasso was born on 25 October 1881 in Malaga, Spain. He died on 8 April 1973 in Mougins, France, at the age of 92. His full Spanish birth name was Pablo Diego José Francisco de Paula Juan Nepomuceno María de los Remedios Cipriano de la Santísima Trinidad Ruiz y Picasso! This name is a combination of Christian saints and family ancestors. Perhaps it may be easier henceforth to use the shorter appellation of 'Picasso', his mother's maiden name, and the one he himself adopted.

Almost everyone has heard of Picasso; even those who do not have any interest in art. This is due to his status in the world as an artist of unparalleled renown during the twentieth century. He famously stated; "When I was a child, my mother said to me, 'If you become a soldier, you'll be a general. If you become a monk you'll end up as the pope.' Instead, I became a painter and wound up as Picasso." Picasso also became famous as a lover. He had many and was married twice: to Olga Khokhlova and to Jacqueline Roque.

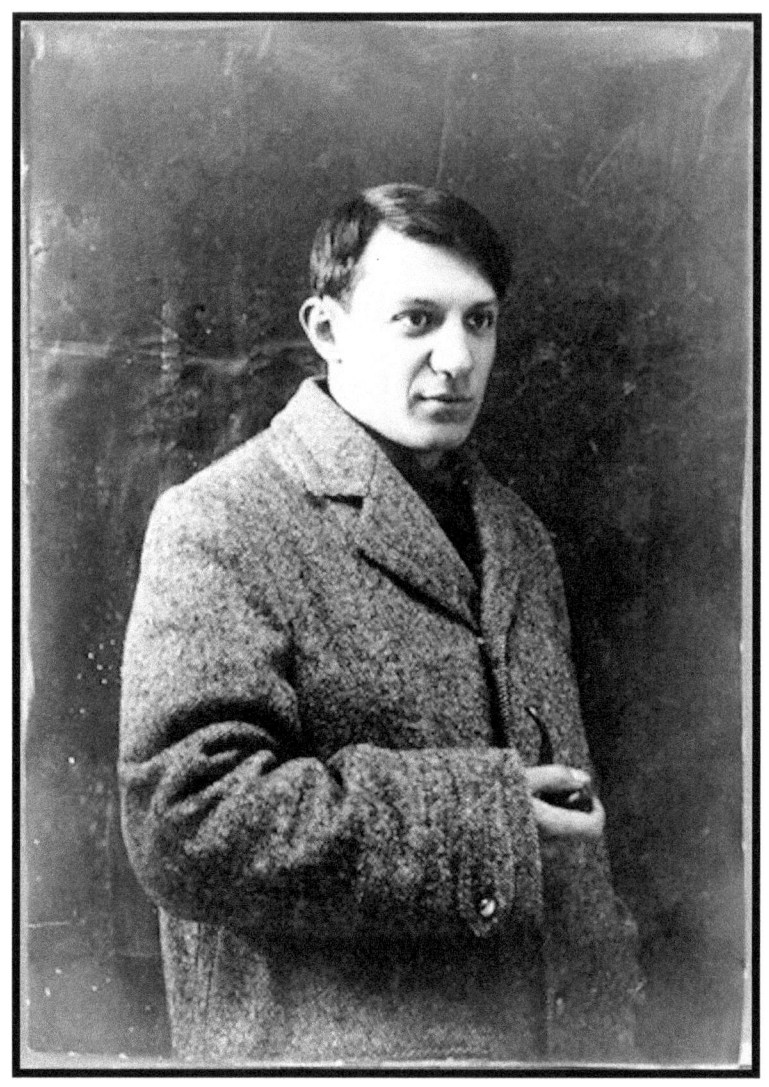

Image 5-1: Picasso in 1908

As a child artist, Picasso was regarded as a prodigy after having been taught by his art professor father. At the age of 9, he created what is now regarded as his first painting known as *Le Picador*. This depicts a man on horseback during a bullfight.

As an adult, Picasso became a prodigious artist, producing somewhere between 20,000 and 50,000 works of art. The overall figure varies, depending on how one counts or defines an individual piece. These works were diverse and consisted of paintings, prints, drawings, sculptures, woodcuts and ceramics. He is probably most famous for his abstract form known as Cubism.

In 1895, when Picasso was just 14 years of age, his family moved to Barcelona, the capital of the Catalonian region of Spain. He was sponsored by an uncle to study there. Upon arrival, Picasso entered the city's prestigious School of Fine Arts. Never one for conformity, Picasso did not readily adjust to the rules and regulations and often did not turn up for class. Instead, he roamed the streets looking for objects to draw.

Two years later, in 1897, the then 16-year-old teenager moved to Madrid where he attended the Royal Academy of San Fernando. This was a prestigious academy and was regarded as the top art school in Spain. Once more, he struggled to conform and was decidedly unhappy during this time.

Picasso moved between Paris and Spain during his young adulthood from 1901 to 1904. This brief period of his artistic life is known as his 'Blue Period'. This term is used to reflect the themes of sadness and loneliness in his work, which included pictures of women, children and street people. He decided to move to Paris some time during the spring of 1904 and settled in the artistic quarter known as 'Bateau-Lavoir'. During 1904 and 1905, his change of domestic scenery was reflected in his work. This is known as his 'Rose Period'. Picasso was inspired by the work of Paul Cezanne and this, together with his friendship with fellow artist, Georges Braque, influenced his work during this period. He lived with Miss Fernande Olivier for a period of seven years during his early years in Paris.

Picasso collaborated with Brasque during the years 1909 to 1912 in order to develop a style that became known as 'Analytical Cubism'. This was a development away from the Renaissance tradition to one that featured more perspectives on the canvas. The next two years, until 1914, were known as his 'Synthetic' phase, often with the use of industrial materials of any kind that fit the mood.

The First World War began in 1914 but Picasso didn't address the war in his work and did not fight it in. There was, however, no legitimate reason for him to fight because his native Spain remained neutral throughout the war. For the whole of the First World War, from 1914 to 1918, he worked in Rome. There, he met his first wife, Olga Koklova; a Russian ballet dancer.

After the end of the First World War in 1918, Picasso paid less attention to Cubism, concentrating more on traditional styles. For the next few years, he adopted the use of images from mythology from Italy's classical period to represent his artistic expression. This period is known as his 'Neoclassical Period' and featured paintings depicting material themes such as his 1919 painting, *Sleeping Peasants*.

In 1927, he began a relationship with Marie Therese Walther, who was just 17 years old when they first met. During the 1930s, and still living in France, he painted voluptuous women, and these paintings displayed a sense of freedom, youth and innocence. The start of the Spanish Civil War in his home nation in 1936 caused him deep dismay. That year, he also met another woman, Dora Maar, who was a photographer. The war produced a number of emotive and powerful works in response. This resulted in the very famous and large mural known as *Guernica* in 1937.

Picasso met a young female painter, Francoise Gilot, in 1943, and four years later, in 1947, she provided him with a child, who they named Claude, and, in 1949 another, Paloma. These were the third and fourth of Picasso's children.

From the latter part of the 1940s, Picasso's output continued and his fame spread throughout Europe and the West. He presented his works in exhibitions in London, Paris, Venice and Tokyo in 1951, and in Lyon, Rome, Milan and São Paulo in 1953. From that point on, interest in his art increased among private collectors and the public in general.

In 1961, he married Jacqueline Roque (1927–1986), when he was 79 years old and she was 35. She was his second wife and remained married to him until he died.

In 1970, one hundred and sixty-five of Picasso's paintings and forty-five of his drawings, produced between January 1969 and January 1970, were displayed at an exhibition in the Palais des Papes in Avignon. These works were mostly of vivacious men and women, often in close embraces.

On Picasso's 90th birthday in 1971, the Museum of Modern Art in New York put on a special exhibition of his works. Simultaneously, the French Government put on a display in the Grand Gallery of the Louvre. This was the first time that the museum had exhibited the work of any living artist.

Picasso continued to work right up until his death, in 1973, aged 91 years, at his hilltop villa of Notre Dame de Vie in Mougins, France, by which time he had become a very wealthy man. He had previously stated, "I think about death all the time. She is the only woman who never leaves me."

Image 5-2: Picasso in his later years

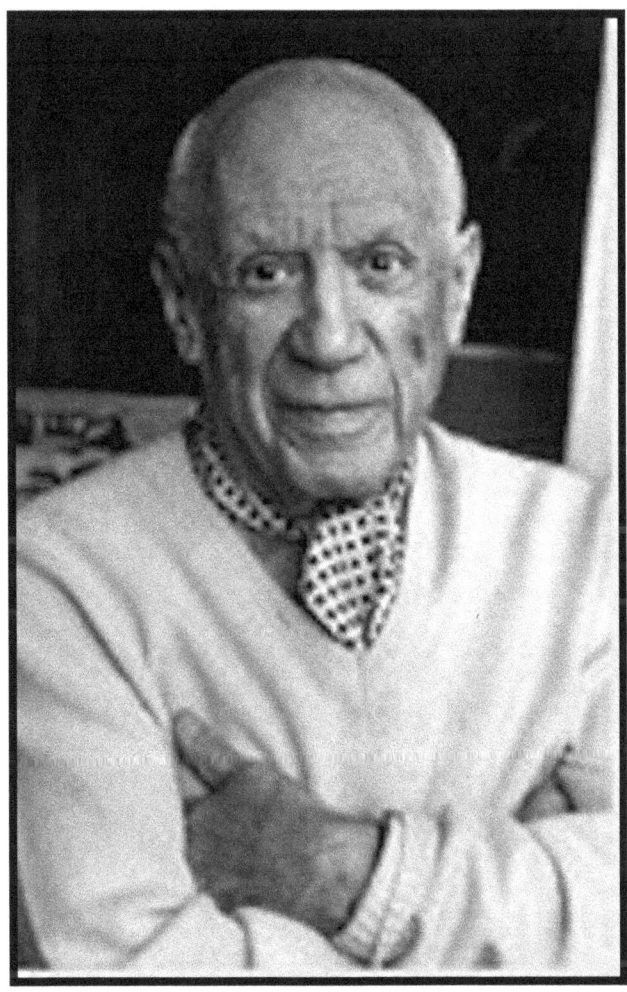

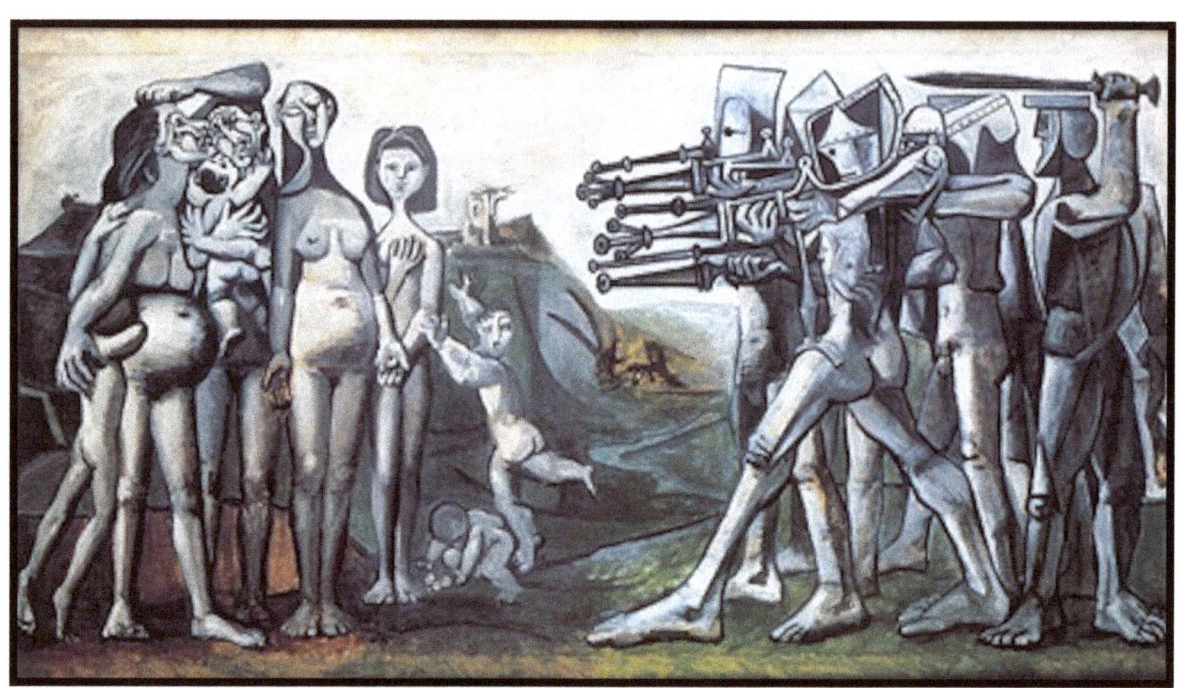
Image 5-3: *Massacre in Korea* (1951)

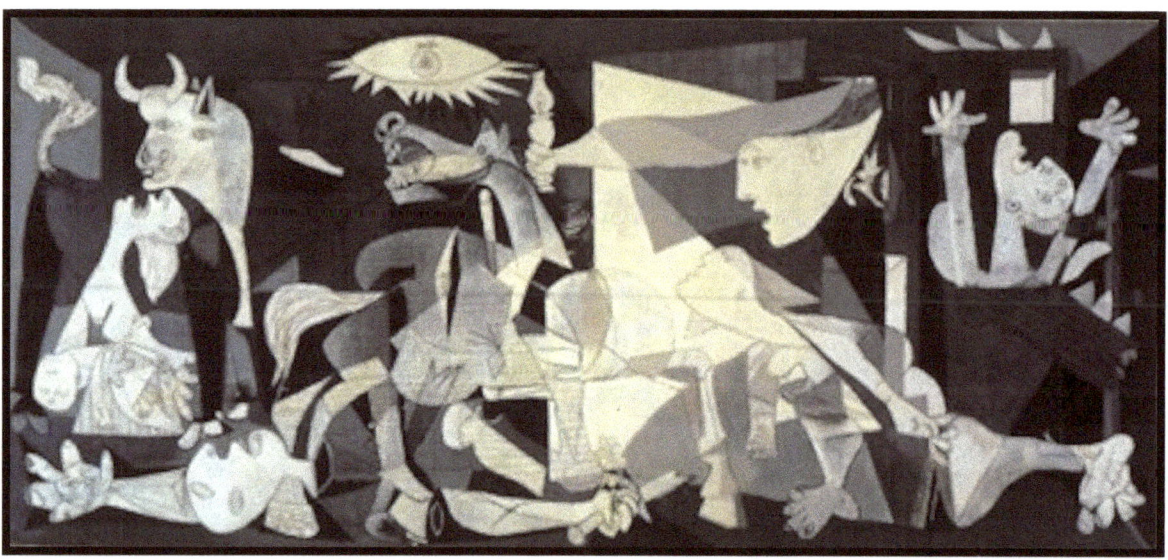
Image 5-4: *Guernica* (1937)

Chapter Six: Pablo Picasso and Qi Baishi – A Comparison

The Chinese Qi Baishi and the Spaniard Pablo Picasso are two of the most representative modern artists of the twentieth century. In recent years, the comparison between Qi Baishi and Pablo Picasso has been regularly made in Chinese artistic circles.

There are many similarities beyond the artists. Both men lived a long life, into their 90s. They were both twice married. Both lived at a time when there were wars within their own countries, including civil wars. Very turbulent times indeed.

Scholars often mention the exchanges between them. In 1956, the Chinese artist Zhang Ting went to France and visited Picasso. Zhang sent a series of Qi Baishi's watermark paintings to Picasso. In July of the same year, the Chinese artist Zhang Daqian met Picasso in France, and the latter showed Zhang his imitations of Qi Baishi's paintings and expressed his great respect for him.

Why did Picasso appreciate Qi Baishi so much? It is probably not just a professional courtesy but reflects a deep respect and admiration.

Perhaps a comparison of the differences between them should also be made from the aspect of the characteristics of modern art. In making a comparison between the modern art styles of the East and West, two of the main characteristics are strengthening the personality and simplifying the form. How is the personality strengthened? That is, to display inner sense and abandon falseness in order to display psychological reality.

Two principle characteristics of modern art in the East and the West are the strengthening of the personality by simplifying the form. Superfluous detail is rejected and the result is a subject whose strong personality and inner sense is given greater clarity.

Although the Eastern and Western styles emanate from different cultural backgrounds and developments, they have similar artistic characteristics. Both Qi Baishi and Picasso are similar characters who strengthen the personality and simplify the form.

Picasso's modern art was rooted in a Western cultural background and development. Personality is a dynamic structure of mind and body that determinates a human's personal behaviour and thoughts. Western society respects individuality and personality.

In modern art, simplifying the form is also a characteristic, as is the strengthening of the personality. The English art critic Clive Bell said, "Simplification is what turns irrelevant details into significant forms. Only simplification could liberate significant forms from irrelevant details."

This is the process of moving from traditional to modern styles. The foundation of modern art is based on Western philosophy. This philosophy can be divided into two types. One is that of Rationalism, represented by people such as Bertrand Russell, Rudolf Carnap, Ludwig Wittgenstein and Karl Popper. It is based on mathematics, logic and semantic analysis, and a scientific methodology.

The other type is Irrationalism, and this is represented by people such as Arthur Schopenhauer, Friedrich Wilhelm Nietzsche, Henri Bergson, Sigmund Freud and Martin Heidegger. This is based upon the psychokinetics of life and intuition and the underlying unconsciousness and use of poetic licence.

From the impressionist perspective, modern Western art generally had two development routes. The first route was that of stressing rational structural analysis. This developed from classicalism to the simplifying form of Cubism, Pure Abstraction and Constructivism and Minimalism. The second route was stressing intuitive self-expression. This developed from Romanticism into Fauvism and Expressionism and into Surrealism and Abstract Expressionism.

The French post-Impressionist artist Paul Cézanne appeared at the juncture of these two routes and was therefore called 'the father of modern art'. He famously stated, "A time is coming when a carrot, freshly observed, will trigger a revolution." In this, he echoed those Chinese Daoist and Buddhist Masters who recommended that one should observe what is, as it is, outside of the concepts of names and avoiding the rational, left-brain type of thinking.

Cézanne's simplified form of geometry opened up the way to Pablo Picasso's Cubism and simplification. Picasso continued Cézanne's enlightened creativity, freely expressing his talents and simplifying the Cubist form of expressionism and surrealism. In so doing, Pablo Picasso became the most influential Western artist of the twentieth century.

Qi Baishi's modern art originated from a Chinese cultural background. This included the Daoist influences of expressing nature in all of its manifestations. To strengthen the personality and to simplify the form are two of the characteristics of modern art that can be set as the criteria to establish whether art is of the modern classification and if it has contemporary operability.

There are some modern influences and elements that exist in Chinese traditional cultural arts. For example, the freehand brush work, especially the free spirit of the Ming and Qing dynasties' literary arts. An example of this is the simple, expressive individuality and simplification of the form that created an extensive space for the development of modern art. Even today we can still appreciate the works of Xu Wei, Ba Dashanren and Shi Tao. This is especially because they have distinct personalities and simply-arranged designs. They create a full of sense of modernity, and it is easy to find an echo of this in modern man.

The Ming and Qing dynasties reflected the last echoes of the feudalistic age in that people's individuality and independence were growing. The well-known poets, Yuan Hongdao and Yuan Mei, from these dynasties, both stressed the importance of personality and 'spiritualism'. Yuan Hongdao said, "To express my emotions without constraint, I only refer to my heart." Yuan Mei also said that all his poems were spiritual. Literary art was also very popular during the Ming and Qing dynasties.

Spirituality was also integrated from poetry to art, especially during the Qing dynasty. For instance, Shen Zongqian said, "I have my opinions and spirit. I'll use ancient methods but will express these in my own way." He stressed the use of a simplified sketch but with vivid and poetic expression. Literary art that obscured the shape but stressed that expression is a progression is similar to the viewpoint of Western impressionism.

Qi Baishi continued with this method of infusing his paintings with spirit and personality and this made him the most influential Chinese modern artist during the twentieth century.

There are four Chinese traditional twentieth-century artists recognised by the Chinese art establishment: Wu Changshuo, Qi Baishi, Huang Binghong and Pan Tianshou. Qi Baishi, the carpenter and folk painter from the small town of Xiangtan, who became a professional artist, was finally accepted in Beijing.

Qi created a 'red flower and ink' style and free-hand flower-and-bird brush work that not only utilised the literary style from the Ming and the Qing dynasties but also absorbed the plain characteristics of folk art. From a refined and elegant literary pattern to a simple and vigorous folk pattern, Qi created a new mode of Chinese modern flower-and-bird painting that has a distinct character and simple sketching full of modern style. Lang Shaojun said that Qi Baishi did not surpass traditional art but that his arts are more modern than contemporary artists.

Qi's style is simple and elegant, his painting is vigorous and energetic, and his style is interesting and vivid. This emanated from his naïve, child-like characteristics, imbued with a sense of homesickness. We can compare the simplistic styles of both Picasso and Qi Baishi.

Picasso used geometric figures to feature an inner structure while Qi Baishi made use of simple sketching and ink to express his inner sense of being. What is more, when Qi was painting fish, he didn't include water. Nevertheless, you can still feel that the fish are swimming. This combination of imagination and reality made Picasso deeply admire Qi Baishi's work.

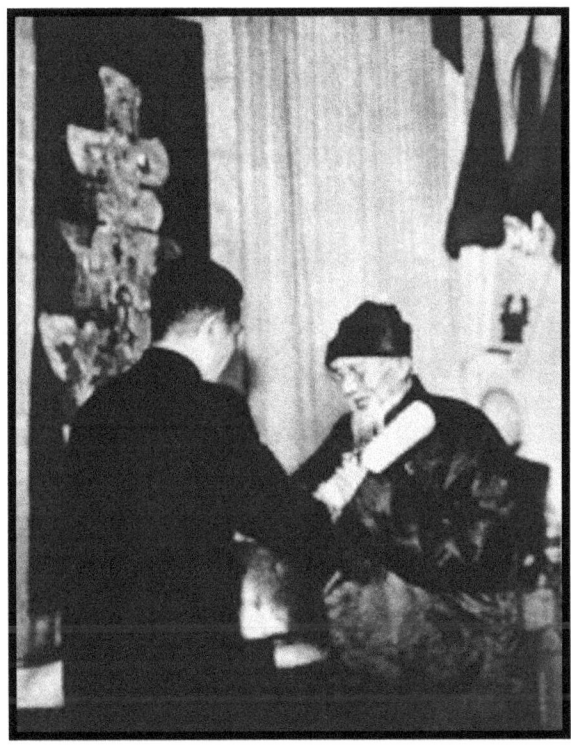

Image 6-1: On 7 January 1953, Qi Baishi was awarded the title of the People's Artist by the Ministry of Culture

Modern Western art strengthens the personality but doesn't strengthen the national character; it balances the individual personality with internationalism. Chinese modern art strengthens personality; however, it strengthens more the national character and indicates the integration between them.

Maybe it is because China has a more 'remote' history and national culture than the

West. If both strengthening the personality and simplifying the form are the common characteristics of both the East and West, then strengthening the national character is the unique characteristic of China.

In China, the belief in what is known in the West as the 'Golden Mean' of symmetry, proportion and harmony cries out against the extremes of self-presentation, revealing psychology and geometric composition. This balance is known in Chinese Daoist thinking as that of seeking balance and harmony. The surrealistic work of artists such as Salvador Dali together with that of the geometric abstract art of Piet Cornelies Mondrian and Kazimir Severinovich Malevich are not readily accepted by the Chinese public. Even when Picasso's Cubism was very popular in the West, there were few Chinese artists who imitated him.

Qi Baishi opined that art should combine reality and imagination and that one should attain a balance between the two modes of similarity and dissimilarity. It seems that Qi's view accords with Chinese modern art's national character and aesthetic taste. Personality and the national character are integrated in Qi's art. His personality increased the national character while at the same time the national character enhanced his personality.

As Qi stated at the award ceremony for the World Peace Grand Prize in 1955, "I love my home town and abundant motherland and all the individual lives. So, I put my ordinary feelings as a Chinese person into painting and creating poems with my whole life and energy."

During the 1950s, Picasso drew lots of doves of peace and so did Qi Baishi. Both experienced wars, so they greatly craved and cherished world peace although they painted different styles of doves representing world peace. Despite the fact that the end of the Second World War was more than 70 years ago, the theme of those doves of peace that were painted by these two giants of the twentieth century are still representative of peace in the world.

Picasso famously stated, "It took me four years to paint like Raphael, but a lifetime to paint like a child." This statement resonates with the Chinese Daoist advice to be childlike and simple, as expressed in Lao Zi's Dao de Jing, 'The Classic of the Way'.

Today, we live in a world where diversity is both recognised and, in most cases, welcomed. Different cultures, ethnic groups, skin colour, religion and social systems exist and, with modern communications, the people of various countries have become members of an intimate community with a shared destiny. There are more than two hundred countries and regions and more than 2,500 ethnic groups following a multitude of religions in the world today.

The stone wall at the entrance to the UNESCO headquarters in Paris carries the inscription of one single message, written in several languages: 'Since wars begin in the minds of men, it is in the minds of men that the defenses of peace must be constructed'. As long as the idea of peace can strike deep roots and the sail of peace can be hoisted in the hearts and minds of people all over the world, a strong defence will be constructed to prevent and stop war.

The dove of peace represents universal human concerns that connect these two artistic giants. Qi Baishi was a man who deeply valued peace. This we can see as a theme through his entire works. He drew a lot of doves as the symbol of peace. Picasso was called 'the father of peace doves'. He also painted a lot of doves in his lifetime but the most famous one is the dove that holds the olive branch that was painted for the Second World Peace conference in the 1950s in Warsaw, Poland. After the Second World War, people longed for world peace, and this became the key global theme during the 1950s.

Picasso's doves were painted flying in the sky, sending peace wishes to the whole world. Qi Baishi began to paint doves in the Chinese way when he was in his 90s. From that time onwards, the dove of peace also became his common subject. In 1952, when the World Peace Conference of the Asia-Pacific Region was held in Beijing, Qi Baishi painted *Flowers and Doves* and sent it to the conference.

In June of the same year, with Chen Banding, He Xiangning and artists in collaboration with another fourteen artists, Qi painted a huge painting called *Ode to Peace*. They sent this to the World Peace Conference held in Helsinki, Finland. Due to the major influence of this painting, on 27 April 1956, the World Peace Council awarded Qi Baishi the International Peace prize. In 1963, he was named by that same body as a world cultural celebrity.

The foundation of Picasso's art is one of rebelling against the traditional Western art style that he was born into. His art was influenced by African wood carvings. Picasso was sensitive and could therefore absorb influences from other countries, such as those that inspired him from Africa and China. He was constantly adapting his methods from the existing way of Western traditional art, and wanted to add new ideas. And so, his outlook expanded into other countries' cultures. When he saw Qi Baishi's album of paintings, he liked them very much and wanted to copy his style.

There are nevertheless some obvious contrasts between Qi Baishi and Picasso. Qi Baishi once talked about the differences between his and Picasso's doves. He said, "If you are painting a dove, you should give it some life, make it affable and then create a peaceful atmosphere. Picasso always painted a dove flapping its wings. I paint a dove not flapping its wings but you can still feel that it is flapping."

The differences between Picasso and Qi reflect those that exist between the two cultures of the West and the East that existed at that time. This contrasts with today, when the world has been made smaller by modern communications and people have willingly adopted the prevailing technology to quench their thirst for knowledge.

Throughout his life, Picasso was constantly adapting his art and was continuously 'discovering the world'. His curiosity always provided him with an opportunity to be creative. He used his techniques to explore the secrets of the world and to establish a new way of expression. This also proved that he was a man who loved life.

Qi Baishi always retained his belief that painting should always maintain a balance. That is, a fluidity between similarity and dissimilarity and imagination and reality. It would, in his eyes, be seen as vulgar if it was too similar to the real thing while it would be regarded as fraudulent if it was too dissimilar. He found significance and beauty in the detail of life when promoting his art. He thus created a simple, unadorned and aesthetically pleasing style of art.

Because both artists presented different aspects and provided subtle nuances of their views of peace, they used their own ways to portray them. Qi Baishi painted the subject of peace through the use of doves by using his own unique method. This is reflected in such paintings as *The Dove of Peace* (1951), *Flowers and Doves* (1952), *Peace* (1952), *Peace Forever* (1952), and *Ode to Peace*. In *Flowers and Doves*, there are all kinds of flowers and doves in flight that create a warm, peaceful feeling. These paintings all expressed a belief that war is not the natural state but rather that peace should be the common pursuit for mankind. The Chinese have long come to appreciate the spirit of harmony and this is a way to express this through the medium of art.

Picasso, however, presents his feelings of where the blame lies for the crimes of war in his art, such as in *Guernica*, produced in 1937, and the *North Korea Massacre* of 1951. In the *North Korea Massacre*, Picasso depicts the terrible massacre committed by the United Nations Command led by America on North Korean civilians. Soldiers are shown pointing their guns at children and pregnant women. Picasso uses this to denounce war and to call for peace.

So, Qi Baishi and Picasso used different ways to emphasise the pursuit of peace. This highlights the differences between the West and the East. These differences are not only in the use of artistic tools, but also in their cultural viewpoints.

On the other hand, Qi Baishi and Picasso had a lot of similar characteristics, both in art and in life. The greatness of Qi Baishi existed in his style, inherited from a Chinese regard for the Dao and reverence for nature and all its objects. In his work, we cannot find anything other than ordinary everyday objects: doves, chickens, vegetables, fruit, and so on. These ordinary animals and plants became the subjects for Qi's paintings. He gave them life and found beauty in ordinary life.

Picasso was always full of energy and creativity. He was seeking justice and truth. After seeking, he found. He used a logical and rational way to depict events and mankind. He was political; he joined the French Communist Party and painted in a way that reflected his anguish. He thereby presented his desire for peace and rejection of war. Qi Baishi used an emotional, Chinese way in contrast to Picasso's use of a rational Western way. The emotional way is from the small to the large, from the microcosm to the macrocosm, which is from the individual to that of universality. The rational way is to move from universality to the individual, from the macrocosm to the microcosm. Both ways point to one aim, which is to represent humanity. So, although these two artists are different, they are both deeply respected by all lovers of art.

Today, doves are used as a symbol of peace, flying out from cages all over the world. Qi Baishi and Picasso, as representatives of lovers of peace from the East and the West, also proved that there are no boundaries in art. The transcendental in art resonates within our hearts.

Chapter Seven: The Qi Baishi Museum in Xiangtan

In present-day China, there is a rich seam of Qi Baishi art and exhibitions. There are three major institutions: the Beijing Fine Art Academy; the Qingzhou Qi Baishi Art Gallery and the Xiangtan Qi Baishi Memorial Hall. There are also many additional research and teaching centres throughout China.

Every three years, there is a Qi Baishi international Culture and Art Festival held in the Qi Baishi Museum in Xiangtan. The Qi Baishi Memorial Hall was originally built in 1993. It is located in the park named after the artist, known as Baishi Park, in Xiangtan City, Hunan. It was rebuilt in 2002 and its total area is 4,360 square metres. It houses more than seventy pieces of Qi Baishi's authentic work. This includes his paintings, calligraphy, seals, poetic prose and wood carvings. There are also exhibits of the works of other famous modern-day Chinese artists. The outside scenery within the park is an appropriate setting for the museum that is fully funded by the Chinese government.

The architecture of the museum reflects a two-level courtyard style. The buildings are made of tiles that look like wood and are based on the traditional architectural style of Hunan. There are flush gable roofs with overhanging eaves, white walls with green tiles, a winding corridor with a courtyard and an indoor pond, with prawn, fish and a fountain. The windows are sculptured with many designs of crabs, shrimps, dragonflies and flowers, in addition to other designs. The inscribed board on the door of the building is inscribed in gold with the words 'Qi Baishi Memorial Hall', written by Sha Menghai.

The museum reflects the life history of Qi Baishi through his works and life events and is well worth a visit. It is located at No. 2 Dahu Road, Yuhu

District, Xiangtan 411100, Hunan, China.

The museum contains a significant display of many original works. There you will find Li Sijin, the co-author of the book, who speaks excellent English and who will be more than happy to show you around and answer any of your questions.

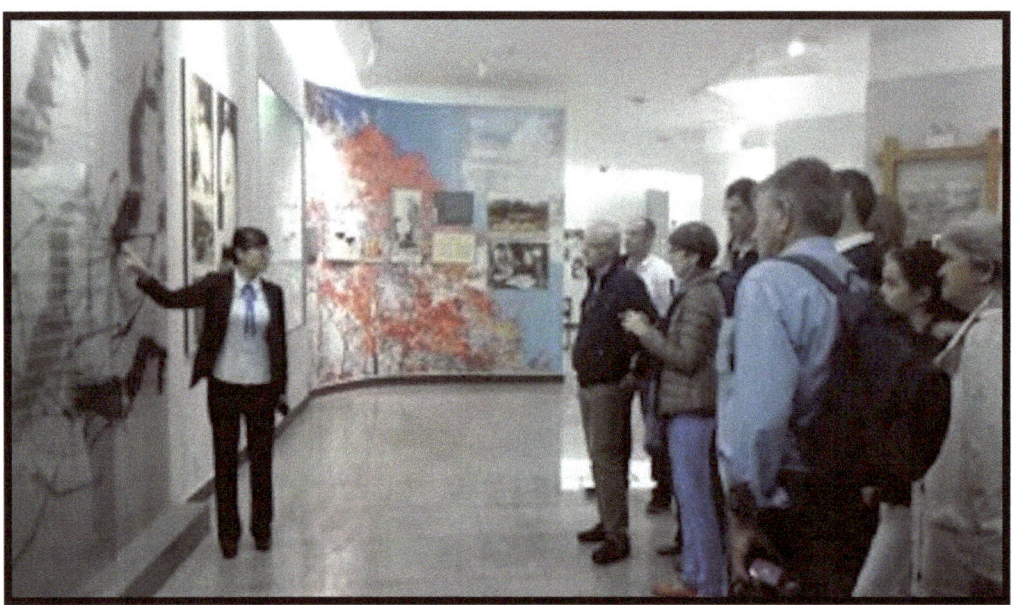

Image 7-1: Li Sijin talking to some tourists at the museum

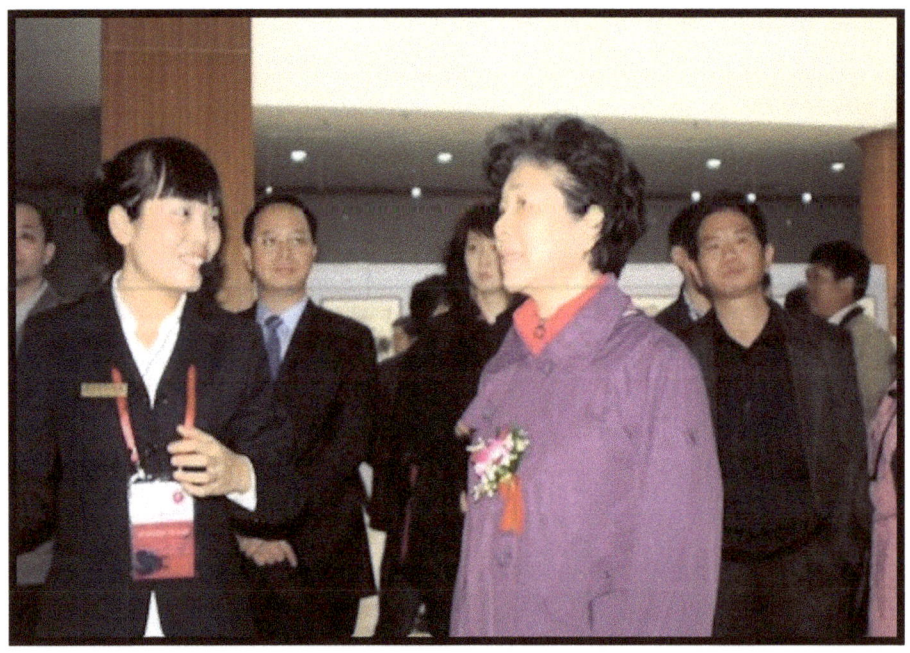

Image 7-2: Li Sijin with government officials from the central Chinese government

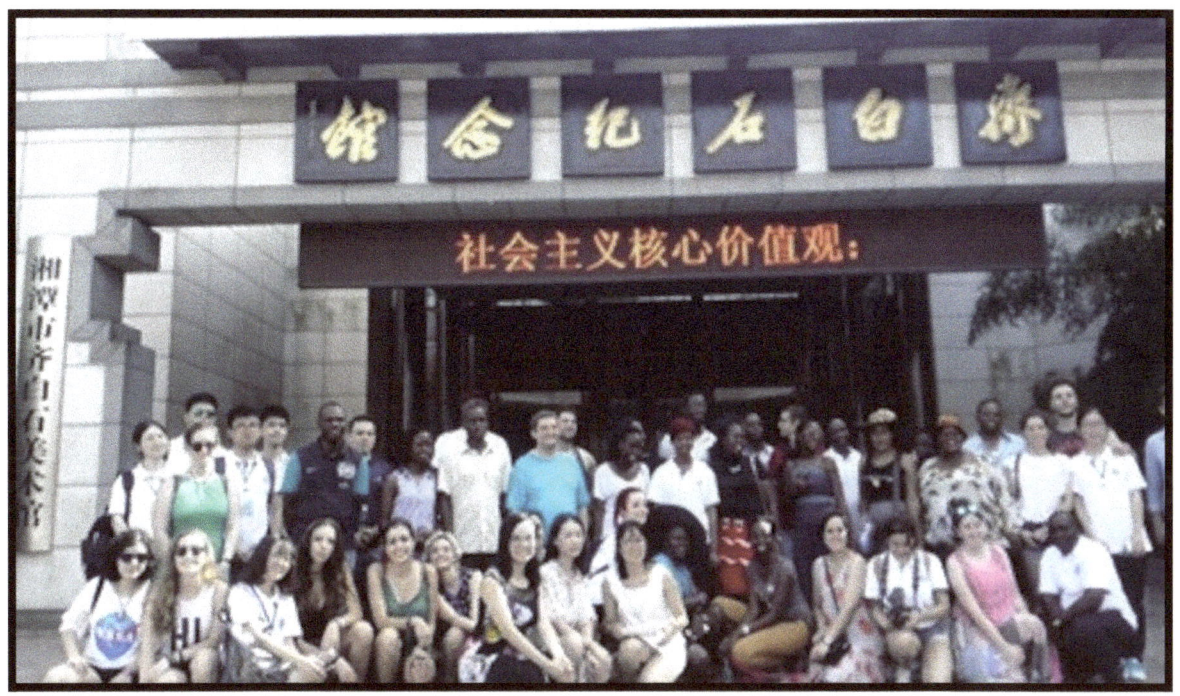

Image 7-3: Li Sijin with some tourists at the museum

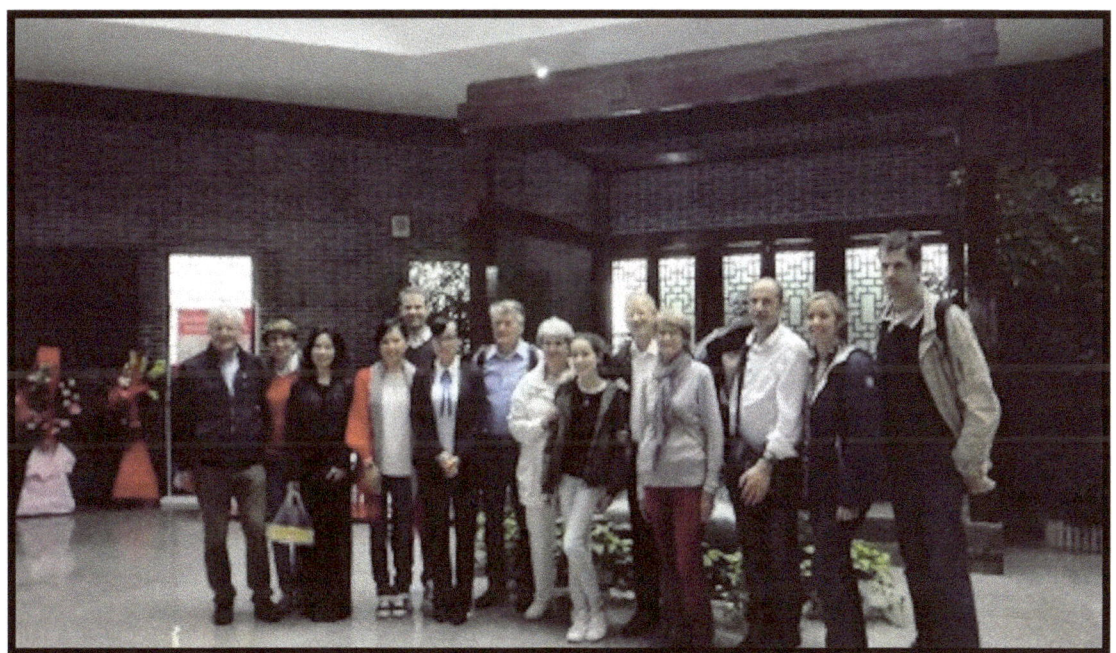

Image 7-4: Li Sijin with some tourists at the museum

On 5 August 2017, there was a special visit made to the museum by the current generation of Qi Baishi's family. They were met by Li Sijin, as depicted in the images below.

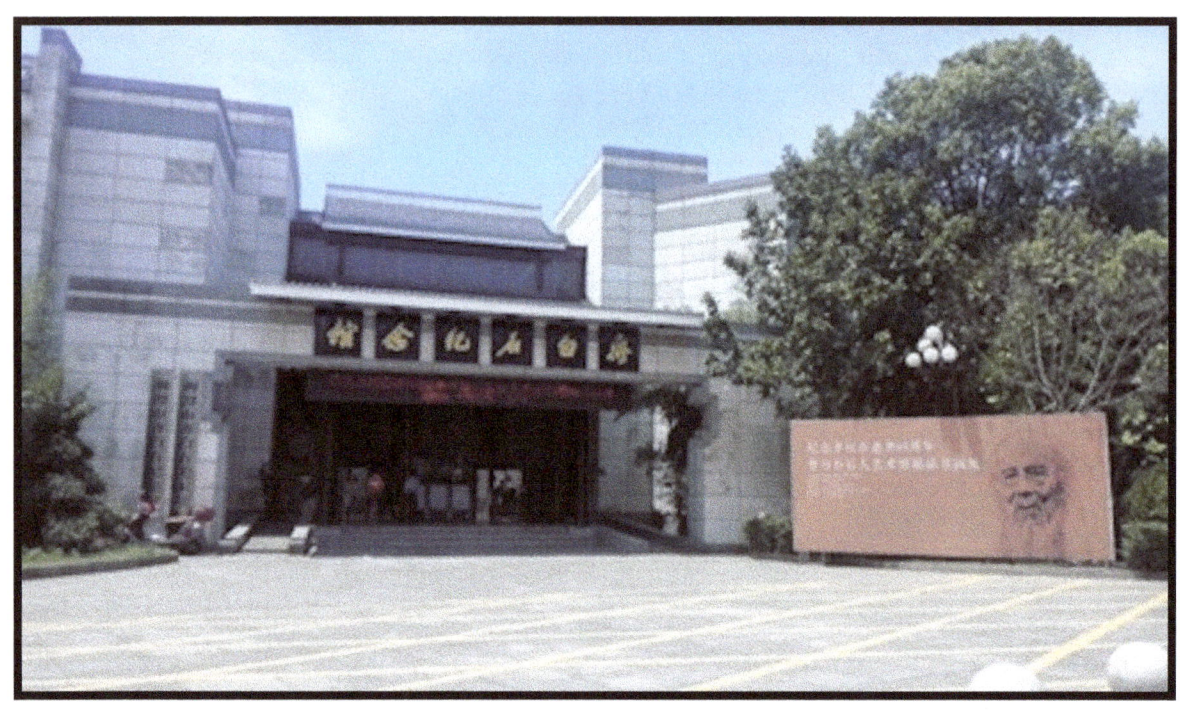

Image 7-5: 5 August 2017 – the museum ready to greet Qi Baishi's descendants

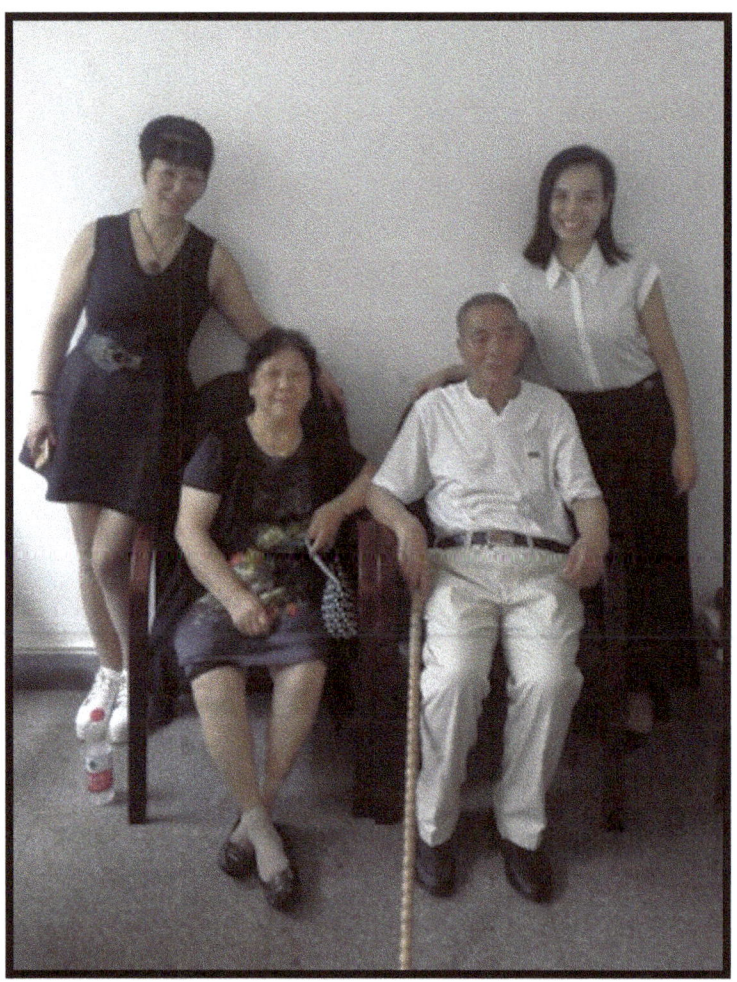

Image 7-6: 5 August 2017 – Qi You Lai (grandson of Qi Baishi) seated with his wife and his daughter (behind) with Li Sijin at the museum

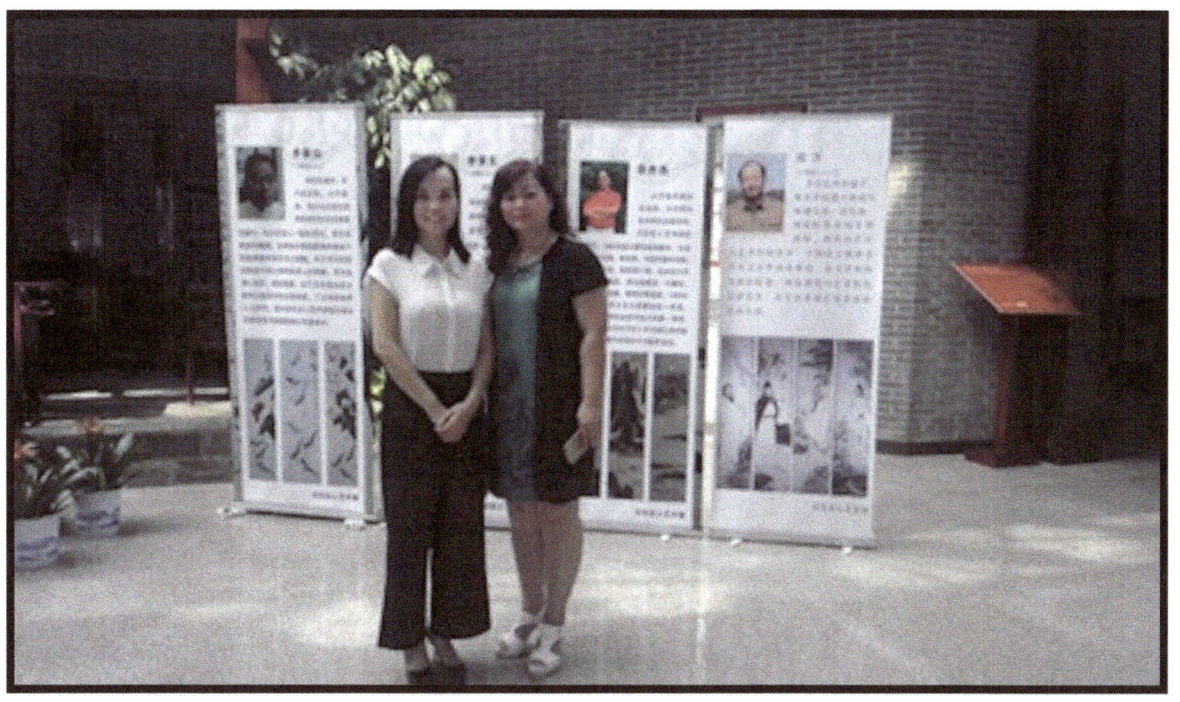

Image 7-7: 5 August 2017 – Qi Baishi's great-granddaughter, Qi Xiaoqing, who is also an artist, pictured with Li Sijin

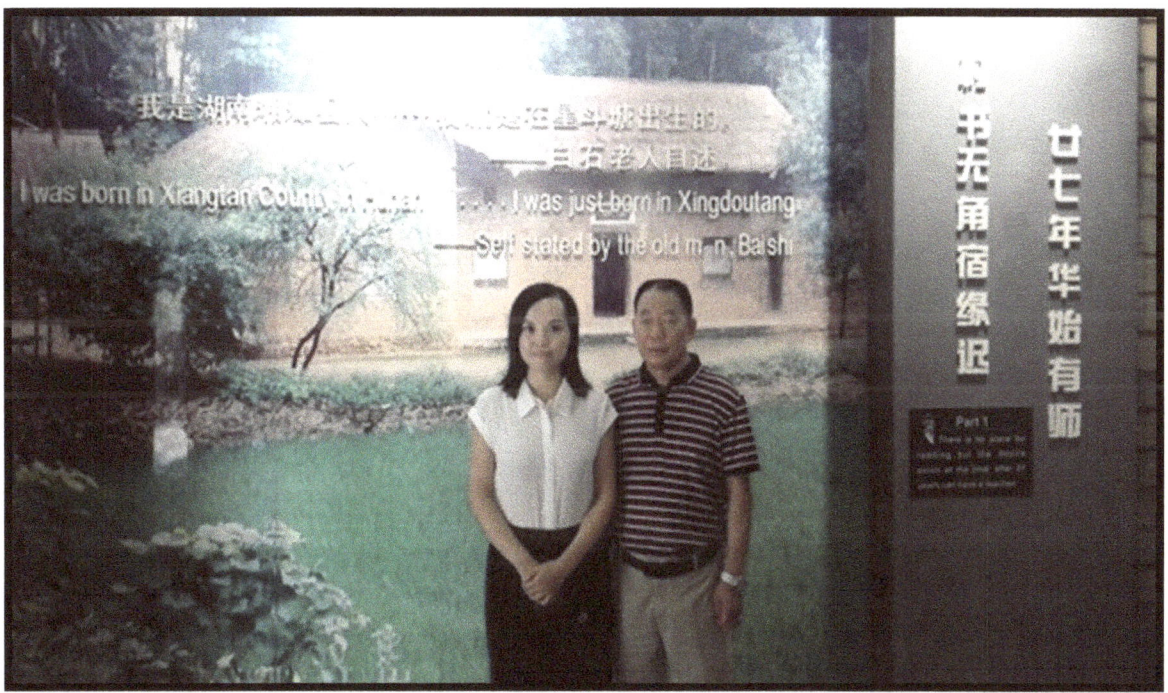

Image 7-8: 5 August 2017 – Qi Baishi's great-grandson, Qi Jingshan, who is also an artist, with Li Sijin

For further details relating to Qi Baishi and other associated traditional Chinese cultural topics, please visit our website or Facebook page:

https://www.taoistartscentre.com

https://www.facebook.com/TaoistArtsCentre/

www.ingramcontent.com/pod-product-compliance
Lightning Source LLC
Chambersburg PA
CBHW041545220526
45473CB00014B/2959